Breakfast at Trout's Place

To Dad,
   Hopefully this book will
inspire another visit.
          Enjoy!
   Love,
      Mike

A writer writes about the country he knows, and the country he knows is in his heart.

—Ernest Hemingway

Breakfast at Trout's Place

The Seasons of an Alaska Flyfisher

Ken Marsh

Foreword by Anthony Route

Johnson Books
BOULDER

Published in the United States by Johnson Books, a division of Johnson Publishing Company, 1880 South 57th Court, Boulder, Colorado 80301. E-mail: books@jpcolorado.com

9 8 7 6 5 4 3 2 1

Cover design: Debra B. Topping
Cover watercolor by Bob White. Prints of the cover painting "Alone Beneath Lake Kulik Spires" is available as a print from Artique Ltd., 308 G Street, Suite 205, Anchorage, AK 99501. Phone 907-277-7459. All proceeds benefit the Alaska State Parks Foundation.

Library of Congress Cataloging-in-Publication Data
Marsh, Ken, 1961–
    Breakfast at trout's place: the seasons of an Alaskan flyfisher /
Ken Marsh.
        p.   cm.
    ISBN 1-55566-247-1 (alk. paper)
    1. Flyfishing—Alaska Anecdotes. 2. Marsh, Ken, 1961– .
I. Title.
SH467.M27   1999
799.1'24'09798—dc21   99-34213
                                                                           CIP

Printed in the United States by
Johnson Printing
1880 South 57th Court,
Boulder, Colorado 80301

 Printed on recycled paper with soy ink

For Sonja, Natalie, and Stephanie

Contents

Fall

Winter

Foreword

Intrepid explorers from all over the world come to Alaska looking for adventure and many of them write about it when they return home. Some of them are talented writers and their stories are fabulous. So fabulous, in fact, that some of us who live here and spend a great deal of time out-of-doors find their words difficult to believe.

Often their bylines are followed with stories about being charged by enraged bull moose and/or brown bears and catching twenty-pound trout while salmon are leaping into their boats, all preceded by a near-death experience during flights in floatplanes.

Certainly we have bull moose and brown bears in Alaska. Huge rainbow trout do exist. There are plenty of leaping salmon, too, and all of us that spend any amount of time flying across the hinterlands of Alaska have had a bumpy flight or a rough landing or two. Lots of the stories, though, are hyperbole.

Often the actual case is that the enraged bull moose was a yearling with diminutive antlers placidly munching on some streamside willows. The brown bear was 300 yards downstream, completely unaware of the upstream angler, and "charged" into the water to grasp a salmon. The floatplane ride, while thrilling for the first-timer, never even came close to upsetting the pilot's can of diet soda.

Without disparagement, I refer to the authors who chronicle these events as one-week-wonders. They come to Alaska for a week and write remarkable stories regardless of what transpired while they were here. They have no benchmark to gauge their experience against the backdrop of Alaska.

Ken Marsh does. He grew up here. That in itself doesn't, however, make him an authority. Anyone can grow up and live in Alaska, but that doesn't mean that they go out and do anything. Ken has and does. He is an authority on Alaska out-of-doors. I've been packed into a floatplane, floated rivers, walked through the woods, and just sat back for the evening in a cabin with him.

What's remarkable about the stories you're about to read is that some are, in a sense, not remarkable. They're just portraits of wonderful days afield. Not every day in Alaska is filled with rutting bull moose, aggressive bears, and an antique floatplane. For that matter, not every day is filled with huge trout and leaping salmon, as you're about to find out.

Fortunately Ken has not only the experience but the ability to eloquently convey in print what it's really like to spend time as an outdoorsman in Alaska.

—Anthony Route
(author of *Flyfishing Alaska*, *Flies for Alaska*,
River Journal—Kenai River)

Acknowledgments

L ife alongside a hard-bitten flyfisher with an "artistic tem-
perament" is an undeniable challenge. This book could
never have been written without the help of Sonja Marsh, my
wife since 1991, whose patience and tolerance have inspired me
and permitted me to write through life's difficult times.

Others who have earned heartfelt appreciation by contribut-
ing to my education as an angler and as an Alaskan (a title held
in this region with fierce pride), include the following: John
Ayres, Greg Landeis, Paul Cyr, Tony Route, David Hagen,
Larry Hagen, Walt Edwards, John Woods, Roy Corral, Tom
Miller, Mark Kufel, Norwood Marsh, Kenneth L. Marsh, and
Sandra Burnett.

Few can write well without reading well. Many contemporary
authors have contributed to this book directly and indirectly.
Some are quoted in the following pages, and most of them have
no idea that I even exist. Nonetheless, I wish to humbly thank
my mentors: Thomas McGuane, Jim Harrison, Russell
Chatham, John Barsness, Nick Jans, E. Donnall Thomas, Jr.,
William Kittredge, Stephen J. Bodio, John Gierach, John Haines,
and the late Norman Maclean.

Thanks also to the editors of the publications in which many
of these stories have appeared, in one form or another: *Alaska*,
Alaska Airlines, *The Anchorage Daily News*, *Flyfishing*, *Gray's
Sporting Journal*, and *Horizon Air*.

Finally, it is true that standing silently behind every successful writer is an editor, or many editors. Many thanks to Jill Sheperd (*Alaska* magazine's long-time ace copy editor), Ron Dalby, Tobin Morrison, Tricia Brown, the late Grant Sims, and John Strohmeyer (editor, professor, and flyfisher). And to Scott Roederer and Stephen Topping for their encouragement, support, and suggestions in editing and publishing this book.

Introduction

Just outside Wasilla, on a hilltop off the Parks Highway, there's a cafe known locally for its home-spun menu and old-fashioned serving sizes. The prices are fair and, far as I know, there's no other place like it within thirty miles of Anchorage. Which is why my wife and I dropped by one March morning for breakfast.

I hadn't been by the place in years, so I wasn't sure what to expect when we opened the door and stepped in. Seated throughout the dining room were a dozen or so middle-aged, flannel-shirted regulars sporting neat haircuts and bill caps. You couldn't tell the truckers from the off-duty cops, or the flyfishers from the bait casters, but I would have been surprised if representatives of each weren't present.

They shot the breeze over ham and eggs, muttering from behind newspapers and steaming cups of coffee, with thundering laughter occasionally breaking the room's moderate drone. Two waitresses bobbed between the tables and the order window, smiling pleasantly. Some of the guys called them by name.

I left my hat on (a pressed-wool Cabela's cap, slightly deformed from summer sprinkles and well-smoked by wilderness campfires) in order to blend in, as Sonnie and I found a table. The subtle charm of the place—the make-yourself-at-home atmosphere, casual dress, and relaxed attitude—was refreshing and reminded me of the older, friendlier Alaska I grew up in. But something else nudged from the periphery.

"Look at all the fish," Sonnie said, as we sat down.

The east wall above the kitchen counter was covered with fish. Big fish. There were Dolly Varden and I think a salmon or two, but mostly they were rainbow trout—several up to five, eight, perhaps ten pounds—mounted on wooden plaques. Mixed in with the mounts were framed color photographs of grinning anglers holding fly rods and large trout.

A waitress appeared and offered us coffee and menus.

"Looks like someone around here likes to fish," I said.

"Yeah," she answered, looking up at the wall, "that's the owner."

My wife asked, "Did he catch *all* those fish?"

"Most of 'em."

"Man after my own heart," I said. "What's his name?"

The waitress's smile fell flat and she stared at me with a deadpan expression.

"Bob Trout."

We moved from Anchorage to Wasilla one month later.

⸺⟨⟩⸺

I don't mean to say I left the big city because of a country cafe that serves real hash browns and caters to anglers. But the little place represented a warmth found in most of Alaska's smaller towns that is long lost in big cities. I missed living in a community where people wave as they pass on narrow gravel roads, where no restaurant or saloon is so fancy that a guy with grease-stained overalls, boots full of sawdust, or a little moose blood on his sleeve isn't welcomed with approving nods.

I'd been hanging by a thread in Anchorage for years. The last night we spent there, the eve of our move, an angry man in a tall red pickup yelled obscenities and nearly ran me off the road in heavy traffic because he had to slow down as I waited to make a left turn. Next morning at 4:30 A.M. I awoke in my old Spenard trailer to what sounded like gunfire near the intersection of Arctic Boulevard and Tudor Road a few blocks away. Sirens of all sorts had wailed throughout the night, as is usual there for weekends. For once, however, the noise didn't bother me.

Raised in pre-oil-boom Anchorage, I remember bears, moose, snowshoe hares, and squirrels regularly passing through our wooded backyard in what was then rural Sand Lake. Cars were fewer, the air cleaner—no brown haze stained the sky over the Chugach Mountains—and on cold January nights you could see the aurora, now often invisible, drowned out by too many harsh city lights.

Things changed fast in the '70s and early '80s, the pipeline years. Spenard Road became a gallery of whorehouses, and the dark, forested acres of south Anchorage and Hillside turned into crowded residential neighborhoods. Dimond Boulevard, once a quiet gravel road, became one of the busiest thoroughfares in town. Suddenly, against my wishes, I'd found myself living in a big, noisy, crowded city.

So Sonnie and I had stepped out of Anchorage for more than a hearty breakfast in quaint digs. We'd left the city for good. Now I can walk under winter stars, where overhead the sky is the color of a magpie's tail, deep blue fading to black, subtly iridescent. I can look to the southwest, maybe ten, fifteen miles across land and sea as the raven flies, and shudder at the nuclear pink and orange glow that lights the horizon as Los Anchorage (as we "locals" call that big city) burns the midnight oil.

I can daydream now about breakup in May, of the trout lakes that sparkle and the streams that dash within minutes of home. I can look up from the desk where I write and tie flies and see *trees* out the window—silver-trunked birches, a few spruce and aspen sprinkled in—and chickadees, redpolls, woodpeckers, and maybe a moose, instead of asphalt. This is Alaska as I've always known it and what this book is really about.

~

If you've ever heard Pete Fountain play "A Closer Walk With Thee" on that golden-throated licorice stick, so sweet, sincerely soulful, and impishly irreverent, or if you've ever watched the film classic *Doctor Zhivago,* where music, scenery, and emotions are blended into poetry, you'll know why sometimes I feel a little claustrophobic working in black and white, paper and ink. Literature is, in so many ways, a limited medium. Still, this is *my* means, the only practical portal to my world.

"Imagine if each day a man must try to kill the moon," wrote Ernest Hemingway. "The moon runs away. But imagine if a man each day should have to try to kill the sun? We are born lucky ..."

And in the end, we are born to be defined by our limitations.

I am an Alaskan, a designation for life that extends beyond geography, that forms my core and forces me to attempt foolish things (such as trying to catch and steal on paper the June sunlight from the Susitna Valley or riffles from the Gulkana River).

Anyone would be fortunate to have grown up as I have, on the fringe of America's dissolving frontier, where even today salmon and caribou outnumber people. I started flycasting here at age four over rising grayling, my rod a badly warped second-hand bamboo. So much of what I've learned since then, about Alaska and about myself, was discovered over long casting sticks on the edges of some of the state's 3,000 rivers and 3,000,000 lakes.

At the moment, it is October, and the season for casting flies is nearly over. But Alaska is full of surprises. Two years ago, the snows came early and fishing was finished by the end of September. Still, warm fronts from the Gulf of Alaska could blow in anytime, as they did last fall, and I could find myself wrestling steelhead on the Anchor River well into November.

Surprises. Years ago, when I was young and still "finding my-self," I worked for a summer at a lodge on the Brooks River in southwestern Alaska. Most of my time was spent washing dishes and making beds, but in the evenings I would fish. One after-noon in late August, a few days before I was to leave for another semester of school, I took a canoe and paddled upriver. Carcasses of red salmon, spawned-out, rotting, littered the gravel bars and a coolness in the air hinted coyly of fall. A brood of mallards, still pin-feathered and flightless, appeared between my canoe and the bank, and I thought I would like to catch one. Just for fun.

I paddled fast, cut them off, forced them onto the bank. The ducklings hustled into grass tall as my chest, and I beached the canoe, hopped out, and gave chase. I made three bold strides be-fore the grass at my toes came alive. Brown bear. I'd nearly stepped on it. The bear had been curled up, sleeping like a wet dog and, for an instant, we stood nose-to-nose, paralyzed. Then the bear, a three hundred-pound two-year-old, wheeled sud-denly, ran a few paces and spun, facing me. The bear started pop-ping its teeth as I backed toward the river, trembling.

When I reached the canoe, I pushed off, running, then leapt in. I paddled downstream frantically for maybe fifty yards, then heard behind me a breathy "*whoof!*" The bear was on the bank standing where the canoe had been, nose in the air, ears pricked. I turned again to paddling, to giving the bear its space, and never looked back.

Alaska can be that way, huckledly-buck between the sublime and the shocking. It is a place of bears and salmon and rainbow trout as long as your arm, a land engulfing thirty-eight mountain ranges—great rock barriers, snow-capped, glaciated, ancient, pristine. And in the shadows of it all flow those wild rivers and uncounted creeks, many never fished.

Over the years I have collected some fish stories, some lasting impressions. Music would lend dimension to their telling, as would the feel of a late summer breeze, cool and damp on the cheeks, carrying the fragrance of a river where salmon run and spawn and return in death to the gravel. But words for now will have to do, will have to try to recreate the hearts of moments spent searching Prince William Sound islands for rare speckled trout; of canoeing buggy muskegs where skulking dinosaur fish tear the lungs out of newly-hatched teal; and of casting for grayling in the Nelchina River basin, those tannic tundra creeks where more than thirty years ago this book truly began.

Such is the intrigue of Alaska, so remote, so real. In its true form, it is not a city or a state of mind, but a place that remains largely wild and raw. It is a place that takes you back in time to a frontier long lost.

One month ago, I spent an afternoon close to home shooting at spruce grouse flushed among falling leaves, followed by an evening on a deserted lake float-tubing until dark for grayling and trout. My friend Mark Kufel had made an unusual shot that day on a black-chested rooster. The bird had flushed between us, and I'd watched, gun at port arms, as the grouse buzzed low over Mark's head. His shot was impulsive, hasty, and on target. The bird fell heavily, a two-pound heap of feathers and wild flesh, and as I traced its hurtling arc, I saw out of the periphery something smaller twirling like a helicopter toward the earth.

Mark already was holding his bird when I reached into the grass and picked up the severed wing. Pointed remarks about *wing*-shooting followed, inevitable as the coming winter. Next bird was mine. It flushed in front of me, flew straight away, and in typical Marsh fashion I missed. Twice.

That evening, as the sky grew thick and inky with hovering clouds, we'd pulled our tubes from Mark's van, traded the shotguns for four-weights, and walked to the lake. The water was still and ringed by fish rising. Mark and I had worked opposite shorelines and I'd used an Adams to stick a few small grayling. At one point, I heard Mark hollering like a loon, his voice echoing over the water and evaporating into the hills scarlet with fall cranberry leaves, tart yellow with birches whispering in a dying breeze. I met him just before dark, when the first sprinkles started falling. He'd caught and released one hell of a rainbow—four pounds, pushing five, the kind that leap and shake and tug your tube around.

Late that night, I returned home in a cold rain to find my pregnant wife, only seven months along, bleeding terribly, wracked by contractions. Horror. Sometime after 1 A.M., in the surreal stillness that preceded sirens, red lights flashing, and reckless driving on wet roads, my second daughter was born. She wasn't much larger than a third-year spruce grouse, though she was slightly heavier—something over five pounds. I've used button-sized flies to catch trout far bigger.

That day defined for me everything that is good in my life: Alaska, this place on the edge, where I live and fish and hunt, the birthplace of my babies. It made me realize that I am living a dream, away from the city, where the world, for now, remains large; where you can pick up your fly rod or shotgun and get away anytime, if only for a while.

Maybe some weekend we'll meet at Trout's Place, that little restaurant just down the road. They serve a great breakfast and, if you like fishing and a little escapism, the atmosphere's tough to beat.

Spring

Desperate Measures

But even in the Arctic winter has an end.
By the middle of April there is no more total darkness.
—Robert Marshall, *Arctic Village*

Last night I dreamed it was spring and that I was flyfishing for grayling, but when I awoke, the room was black. I reached out and touched the window pane—it was cold as ice. Outside, smoky clouds muted a full moon. Old snow clung like Styrofoam to the ground, and I knew that it was still January and that I was still in Alaska.

Around this time every year, it's the same: you're ready to fish but winter stands in the way. So you learn to find nourishment in dreams, to console yourself into fitful contentment the way a starving prospector might eat boiled shoe leather.

Alaskan winters are measured by anglers in terms of darkness and confinement and by the number of flies tied by May, when daylight returns and the ice dissolves. The darkness is a toxin to which few—including those of us who've spent our entire lives north of the sixtieth parallel—ever grow accustomed. It's like breathing exhaust in an auto shop: oppressive, noxious. You can ignore it only so long before one day—or one winter—the poison accumulates. In the case of too many Alaskan winters, seasoned sourdoughs (folks who've soured on Alaska and finally have the dough to leave) burst into seizures and check out to trailer parks near, say, Phoenix or Las Vegas.

Figure, though, if you can hang on until March, that long, heart-wrenching tease of a month, there will be hope. One afternoon the eaves will weep as winter appears to die, drop by silver drop. Next morning you'll awake smiling, only to find heavy frost trimming the windows. Half a foot of fine, fresh snow will cover the old hard stuff, and you'll spend the day looking out at a universe of twirling flakes, wondering when it will ever stop. Winters here die hard. They test your sanity.

I drove by the Little Susitna River last weekend—one of the upper reaches off Fishhook Road southwest of the Hatcher Pass turnoff. Cold as it was, the land snow-covered and the river hidden beneath tons of ice, I spotted some open leads. Which got me thinking …

In its lower reaches the Little Su hosts thriving runs of king and silver salmon, both liberally "enhanced" by the Alaska Department of Fish and Game. Thousands of local and visiting salmon anglers mob the state access sites each summer. And they do pretty well. But the lower stretch isn't really for flyfishing. There the river runs deep and slow; birch trees and alder brush crowd the banks making backcasts difficult. And there are too many salmon-crazed people hurling hardware to really make a roll cast pay.

The upper river, though, pours from a steep, narrow, alpine valley, bouncing and dashing among boulders the size of garden sheds. Hatcher Pass Road parallels the upper river, and I'd heard that in the pools you can catch goldenfins—stunted, resident Dolly Varden, six to eight inches long.

It's that stretch off Fishhook Road, the place where I spotted the open leads, black and roiling amidst a frozen winter desert, that now has me wondering. Even in January you can see that the upper Little Su has all the ingredients of a fine trout stream: cottonwood- and white-spruce-lined, drift heaps here and there, tall cutbanks flanking its south side and gravel bars on the north. In the summer I've noticed shallow cobble riffles pouring sprightly into dark pools; mud-bottomed beaver channels hide treacherously below chest-high hanks of summer grass. I've known big rainbows to hang around the mouths of such channels in other rivers.

Certainly some of the salmon that slip the mobs must travel up this far. I'm aware of no major obstacles. And, of course, where there are salmon, there are scavengers. Dolly Varden, rainbow trout, and grayling follow salmon the way wolves shadow caribou herds. When salmon spawn, the scavengers snap up stray eggs. Later, after the adult salmon have spent themselves and hang white and rotting in the current, rainbows and Dollys tear off flesh in ragged chunks, shaking their heads like little sharks.

Yet I've never heard of anyone fishing this part of the river. Particularly in January. So now I'm crotch-deep in snow—deep enough that this morning's powder is sifting into the tops of my hip boots—and I'm thinking how stupid I'll look if someone spots me.

Alaskan flyfishers may be the toughest of a breed; you've got to be a little hard-headed to remain enthusiastic about a sport that is as transient as the state's brief summers. But we make the best of it here by fishing twice as hard when the sun climbs high and the ice disappears.

By April the tension is palpable. The creeks start opening up and word will have it that the boys way down south on the Situk River are into some serious steelhead. Snowstorms continue to be a possibility, but winter's end is in sight. Harbingers appear daily—patches of bare ground showing under spruce trees, a pair of Canada geese eating yellow grass exposed on a highway median. Every week I'll be checking a lake close to home where sixteen-inch grayling strike Marabou Lake Leeches cast into the first open leads.

Back in my truck, above the Little Susitna River, I'm shivering even as the defroster blows full blast. A cold front's settling in and the riffles are closing up. The day is growing dark already and, for the moment, spring and flyfishing remain out of reach, still a third of a year away.

I guess it was a foolish move, visiting a frozen river in January with a fly rod. But desperate times call for desperate measures. And, what the heck, if I hadn't gone, I wouldn't have gotten the exercise and likely would have loafed around the house, reading fishing magazines or tying more flies.

Alaskans must have diverse imaginations and learn how to improvise. These are prerequisites, never more apparent than in the heart of winter when you realize that, for someone with a one-track mind, four more months is a long, long time to wait.

March Madness

The snowshoe hares are running amuck, black-eyed hermits suddenly aroused, victims of hormonal swings brought on by the celestial magic of early spring. They dance in the moonlight over crusted corn snow, kick-boxing with clownish hind feet, their desperation marked on the four-lane between Wasilla and Anchorage by twisted carcasses, downy-white and bloodspattered. No risk too great for that one, scintillating thrust.

We call it March madness. And the fly rods and reels packed in the back seat of my car suggest that madness is not limited to horny hares. It's been a long, fishless winter.

I'm thinking as I drive to the airport about the flight to King Salmon, about soaring hundreds of miles over a world that is cold, colorless; a lifeless melding of black and white, etched in transparent evening light. This is more a season for hunting ptarmigan, the white willow grouse stalked on snowshoes over hard-packed drifts. (The ptarmigan's call is mocking, resembles a human laugh that is at once nervous and petulant, hoarse. When it comes from your back or follows your side-by-side's second shot, it is a voice that burns.) But this is no bird hunt. Right now I must envision a river—ice-free, flowing emerald-green through a stark tundra plain—and Mac Minard, my friend from Dillingham with a tumbler of twelve-year-old scotch, all waiting barely an hour away.

King Salmon is an outpost of rusted steel, chipped paint, and compact buildings—modular, single-level, all begging for a good wire-brushing and fresh latex. People here are friendly, they nod and say hello to perfect strangers passing along gritty gravel alleys. The Naknek River's lower reaches hustle with the tides past the town's fringes, hauling icebergs in and out from Bristol Bay where walruses live. Strangely enough, the place also boasts an unlikely cosmopolitan edge. Talk of the town a few years back: actor Tom Hanks appeared at the airport, strolling over the gray tarmac from a private Leer jet that he flies himself. Passing through on his way to Asia, Hanks is said to have spent an hour under the scrutiny of gathering local eyes, sipping an espresso in a local cafe while attendants refueled his plane.

Mac's waiting at the airport with wind-burned cheeks and news of a day spent on the upper Naknek. River's open, days are mild and pleasant, the rainbow trout fat and taking streamers— Woolly Buggers, big, black, ugly #2s, and Bunny Leeches long as your index finger. The scotch is waiting.

Dawn. The hills beyond the river are lost in ice fog, the neck-high willows and dwarf arctic birch trees flocked in hoar frost. Mergansers and goldeneyes, life imitating art in black and white, sail over the river through dawn's muted silver light. Mac offers a word of caution: look out for drifting ice chunks while wading. Thousand-pound pans ride silently and low in the current. Sneaky. They'll stalk you from behind, he says. Had one yesterday nearly take him out at the knees. You don't want to swim the Naknek right now. Thirty-eight degrees. It'll suck the life out of you.

The boat, a flat-bottomed river-runner with a forty-horse jet, slides off Mac's trailer, onto crumbling shelf ice and into the river, green, translucent—you can see cobbles on pool bottoms fifteen feet deep. A mile upriver, the Naknek slips out from under the ice of Naknek Lake, Alaska's fourth largest with 242 square miles of surface area.

I once spent a summer on the lake, working at a lodge where

the Brooks River feeds in. Days off were few, but when I could, I would wrangle a skiff and outboard and buzz over to the Bay of Islands thirty-some miles east of where I stand today. Mostly I would troll plugs—big silver monsters—and catch lakers, arctic char, northern pike, and trout. Caught many fish better than ten pounds, puttering around in the skiff on summer evenings among islands that glowed in the tangerine fire of a low-slung sun. Finally I would boat a small laker, then camp on an islet out of reach of prowling brown bears. Nights were spent next to alder smudges, eating fish baked in buttered tinfoil and lemon, sipping Jack Daniels, and listening to loons calling.

But the lake this morning remains locked up, frozen, and my fishing will be done on the river, from gravel bars, using a long rod and feathered hooks. In a moment, the jet unit is purring, *bub-bub-bub*, exhaust salting the clean, freezer-locker air. Then Mac opens 'er up and we're gliding downriver, among the winging ducks.

Only weeks ago, in the dead of winter, Mac had called and proposed this trip. No one flyfishes remote southwestern Alaska in March. But Mac is the regional sportfish biologist. He knows this place, knows when and where to find big rainbow trout. So I am here, a little stunned, ready to cast over the first really ice-free stream I've seen in five months.

Noon. I'm standing thigh-deep in a tailout casting a heavy Black Bunny Leech into a seam forty feet out. The fog's burned off, a white horizon surrendered to pale blue ozone. Still, everything on the river remains silver: leafless shrubs in fuzzy frost coats, brittle ice forming in my guides with each cast. And then, with a tug that surprises and pleases me, I'm into a four-pound rainbow trout, bright as polished chrome, running, thrashing, following my leader to be plucked, eventually, from the chill of the quick-silver run.

In a moment the fish is gone, released, and already I'm considering the wonder of it all, that cold-blooded creatures can possibly live and function in a world so completely without heat. I can smell on my hands the summer fragrance of rainbow trout, a suggestion of fennel and thyme mixed with crushed river grass. Then Mac hoots and I look upstream where he stands above a stony chute, rod bowed over his head like a halo in that sterling March light.

The beauty of this river, like so many others in this part of Alaska, is not that you can catch rainbow trout in March, but that you might at any time catch a trout of incredible size. That summer working at the lodge, I once saw an enormous trout hanging by its jaw from a scale. Killed by a tourist, the trout missed twenty pounds by just a few ounces. Our biggest today weighs probably around eight pounds. It's a buck, dark-bodied with white-tipped fins, a pre-spawner preparing for April and pea-gravel redds. Mac catches it on a Woolly Bugger, and as he lets it go, I cannot help thinking how much this whole affair—the eight-weight rods, sinking lines, gaudy streamers, something about the trout themselves—resembles fishing for winter steelhead.

In fact, rumors of trout caught in saltwater off the Naknek's mouth in commercial salmon nets and of bright river fish sporting sea-lice have led to whispered debates about a local steelhead run. Mac says the rumors are false. Sure, it's likely that some trout venture into brackish water, chasing and feeding on ocean-bound salmon smolt. But the life cycle of these rainbows is connected solidly and completely to the great lake and to the twenty-six- to twenty-eight-mile stretch of river leading to the sea. The trout here grow large because salmon eggs and salmon carcasses, high-protein provender, are plentiful throughout the summer and fall. Young salmon maturing in Naknek Lake provide solid forage all winter long.

Still, if you awoke suddenly one March morning on the Naknek with a steelhead outfit in your hands and a thrashing fish out front, you might think you had died and gone to heaven and that heaven is a tundra stream in late winter full of deep-bellied steelhead trout.

Evening arrives suddenly, on the hooves of four white caribou trotting along the shelf ice near the mouth of Naknek Lake. They skip like African springbok, in single file, into the green glass river, four bovine heads, bug-eyed, swimming in a serpentine chain to the far side, onto the gravel, bouncing over a windblown, snowless tundra of umber and burnt sienna, pausing among white puffs of willows to shake beads of ice from their warm, hollow-haired coats.

Mac's backing the boat trailer down the launch, and for the first time in ten hours, I'm looking forward to evening at the local bar and grill. We'll have beer and burgers big as your face, served by a paunchy giant sporting a Fu Manchu mustache the color of old Wesson oil and wearing the same grease-stained T-shirt he'd perspired in serving breakfast the day before. Then it'll be back to the bunkhouse for single malt scotch and Mac's intensity—monologues detailing catch quotas, growth statistics, migration theories. Biology and fisheries management according to Mac.

I'd fished the Naknek once, eight years before in October, following a storm that encased the willows in ice, left them sparkling and prismatic in the sunshine that followed, a billion blazing gems. I'd fished with a local school teacher named Peter Bakun, a Montana transplant who to this day spends every moment possible flyfishing the Naknek. I don't recall a lot about that day, other than the frozen wind screaming off the tundra and my red, raw knuckles. We'd fished a stretch that locals call "the rapids," caught plenty of fish, mostly Dolly Varden to two, three pounds and big grayling, the color of spruce ashes, with tall, webbed dorsals. Peter, wearing a bushy beaver-fur cap, had stuck a couple of rainbows, smallish, maybe two pounds, no bigger than the egg-sucking Dollys we'd caught on Glo-bugs.

Back then, says Mac, the rainbows were fewer and smaller on average than those in the river today. Too much fishing pressure, too little catch-and-release made ten-pound fish rare. Since then, the Naknek has been managed as a trophy rainbow fishery. Trout-hungry locals can take a fish or two under sixteen inches on baitless single hooks, but larger fish must be released. Tomorrow, Mac says, we will fish the rapids.

Temperatures at night fall into the twenties, but by late morning the air has warmed considerably. Still, it seems odd to find stoneflies hatching and crawling over banks of rotting ice. The stones are small, black, slender as twigs, and no longer than a fingernail. I'm hiking down a half-mile stretch of dry cobbles, stumbling, by-passing the rapids to reach a likely pool below.

Mac's upstream in the boat, dropping off a pair of friends who have joined us for the day. My belly is full of greasy eggs flipped an hour ago by the beer-bellied giant (same T-shirt). He'd had help this morning, a young waitress, plump, cheerful, with sweet dimpled cheeks. Mac had asked her if the big guy speaks.

"Oh, that's Bubba," she'd said (a name we'd already guessed). "He's not as mean as he looks…but he *has* been in prison."

Southwest Alaska, isolated, all but roadless—a place literally on the edge—is something of a Wild West. It is a region where notoriety can dissolve into anonymity, one of the last places on earth where a man can go to escape a sticky past. You never know who might be flipping those eggs on the far side of the order window or how many states he might be wanted in.

Mac and I agree. It'll be *Mister* Bubba from now on. Just to be safe.

Black, buggy flies aren't doing much this morning, so I've tied on something different: fluttering purple bunny-fur strip over pearlescent Mylar body; a pink chenille head. Grotesque, but flashy. I figure in water this cold, those fish may need all the stimulation they can get. By late morning, I'm casting to a slick where the rapids spill into a great, troubled pool. Seventy yards wide, forty long. Big water. But this is the only pause for a half-mile in each direction. It is a good place to find trout resting.

An early cast provokes a sharp pluck, like a metal pick on a banjo string. Then nothing. I'm throwing a sink-tip, a twenty-four-footer, heavy but smooth. It hangs up on rocks now and then, a good sign that the fly is getting down where it belongs. A couple more drifts and I'm hung up again. I lift the rod, yank upstream to pull my streamer free, but this time I sense a bouncing give. Then my line screams downstream, alive, trying desperately to escape. In an instant, the rock has become a ten-pound trout—stubby, thick, heavy like a chunk of stovewood—leaping over the riffles, once, twice.

I've tailed the fish inside of ten minutes, a buck pushing thirty inches, shovel-nosed, broad-shouldered, freckled like a leopard with red-blazed flanks. It's sliding back into the pool when Mac roars up in the boat, asks if I want to join him across the river. But I'm fine right here, so he roars off and soon I can see him over the roiling current, casting off the far side.

In a minute I'm into another fish, this one bigger than the last, a creature terrified. All I can do is shout and hold on and watch the line melt off my Lamson, hope that those strong cold-

blooded shoulders wear out before I run out of backing. They
do, and soon I'm gaining on a thrashing storm. Thirty inches,
twelve pounds. Easy. Mac's hollering over the current, "*The
flyyy. What colooor?*"

More fish wait for me in that pool. Three trout—an eight-
pounder, another around five, and a gravid, six-pound hen the
color of steel in sunshine—and a grayling close to two pounds.
By the end of the day, the point's been made. Everyone's caught
fish better than ten pounds. Purple was the color. No one knows
why. Mac confesses over dinner that he'd fished that rapids pool
two days earlier, the one where I'd found the grayling and five
trout of my dreams, fished it for hours without a touch. You just
never know.

The final morning is a windy son-of-a-bitch, the kind that
snatches your cap and rolls it across the tundra. We're gathered
down at the launch, along with a pair of guides—one a pretty
woman, petite, with a hot-pink cap. Her partner, a sad, bearded
man, follows her with eyes that seem strangely haunted. They're
herding a group of clients from Phoenix. The sports are happy,
fresh, with golf-course tans and name-brand clothing. The guides
resemble Mac and I: wind-burned faces, chapped and red, crow's
feet clawing past dark Polaroids. Word has it that the guides once
were sweethearts, until the woman learned the river. Now it's
strictly business. At least, as far as *she's* concerned.

Sometimes I think guiding in Alaska must be a tough way to
make a living. Beyond the implicit glamour, there is little more
than weeks of watching and accommodating, trying to uphold
big expectations. It's bad form to fish in front of clients. Instead,
you show them the best water, help them tie on their flies, shrug
helplessly when a two-hundred-dollar day comes up fishless, or
virtually so. You're out from dawn to dusk in wind and grayness,

raw from it all, dehydrated, headachy. The guides will tell you it beats growing fat and sleepy behind an oak desk. Still, they earn their money.

The outboard's chugging again and we're backing off the launch. I look up and see the woman in the pink hat waving. Behind her, the man with the haunted eyes is watching sadly.

A good part of the day is spent searching for bends out of the wind. We catch a couple more trout, smaller ones today—three, four pounds apiece. Brings us back down to earth. There is lunch on the tundra, next to a frozen bear trail, cold cuts and cold beer on a raw day. And then the fishing's over and we're back at the launch, loading up the boat one last time.

We're tying things up when the wind changes direction, lightens up a bit. It feels almost warm. I wonder if perhaps I'm only getting used to it. Then Mac spots three dark, misty puffs on the horizon over the river. Geese, he says. New arrivals. They're here to chase winter away. I'm starting toward the truck, but something tugs at my feet. There's a loud, sucking sound that makes me look down. And there it is. My boots are sticky with brown, sloppy mud. Spring is officially here.

Gulf Coast Secrets

W e are turning on the wing of Steve Ranney's Cessna, low, like a mechanical eagle whose insides are living things that see and shout.

"There's your river," Ranney hollers. (His name has a phonetically appropriate ring for a Gulf Coast pilot.) The river is beautiful, even through veils of wind-driven rain, coursing through a trackless wilderness unchanged since before the Mayflower, Columbus, the Vikings.

Ranney circles for my benefit, allows me to study the topography—a miserable expanse of tidal marsh, alder thicket, and forest—then straightens out and heads for a range of sand dunes bordering the distant Gulf of Alaska. There will be only one way to reach the river: bushwhack from the ocean across a brackish lake, through two miles of waste-deep bog, then past the clinging alder jungle.

We're dropping into the dunes within two minutes, a trip that on foot will take me that many hours. A crude airstrip appears among sand hills two stories high, and soon we've bounced to a stop and everything is still except for the wind and the rain splattering the side of the plane.

Of course, I'm anxious, eager to fish in the wake of another long winter. But something else excites me even more: that river beyond the marsh and the alders is an enigma. State biologists know that 50,000 silver salmon spawn there each September and that three times that many are taken by commercial gill-netters at its mouth. But beyond that, the river is biologically uncharted, a great unknown. Still, there have been rumors. A friend who once made his living netting salmon in the area muttered that big sea-run trout sometimes appear in the mesh. They're quietly tossed in with the silver catch and sold by the pound, he'd said. Steelhead. Everybody seemed to catch a few.

Now it's late April, and the dunes, the gulf, and that river running through the middle of nowhere are deserted. No salmon, no people. In my duffel there is an eight-weight rod, a reel, and several boxes of flies. In my head a question throbs, and there will be no relief until I've attacked it head-on.

Ranney leads me a stone's throw from the surf to a drafty shack atop a dune. He uses a claw hammer to wrench nails from the weathered plywood door and apologizes for the shack's rusticity. But when the rain falls and the wind blows (actually, a friend familiar with the region once warned that the wind here never blows, it *sucks*), a plywood shack—and this one comes complete with a functional oil stove—becomes a castle. No apologies necessary.

I've hauled my gear up from the plane—fly rod tube, waders, a cardboard box of food—and Ranney is bending his six-foot, two-inch frame back into the Cessna. In a moment, he will roar off, over the dunes and the black, tossing sea. And for the next four days, I will be on my own.

Alaska's Gulf Coast is wet, windy, and remote. Ocean squalls pile into glacier-hung mountains, and the wind sometimes howls for weeks without pause. On rare mild days in spring and summer, when the sun shines and the hemlocks dry out, it is a place of harebells, salmonberries, and creatures as delicate as thumb-sized rufous hummingbirds. The deltas of several great rivers provide avenues for salmon—awesome runs of sockeyes, kings, and silvers—and serve biannually as funnels for birds migrating by the millions. But more than all that, the Gulf Coast is wild, a place where unfished streams purl as unanswered questions, beyond the ken of biologists and anglers, through unspoiled valleys.

The surf advances with a drum roll that crescendos, peaks, then breaks and retreats in a carbonated hiss. It is late afternoon and I am leaving Ranney's shack, clad in waders and rain gear, fly rod in one hand. I'm walking inland, through a steady rain, across the dunes. Here and there, canine prints wide as my hand show crisply among the wet dunes. Wolves.

I'd spotted several moose laying among the alders as we'd flown in. The moose are safe from wolves today since the snow-pack that bound them, that left them floundering helplessly, has melted. The wolves have been forced to move out to the dunes where they can make their livings by the mouthful, snapping up voles and migrating birds.

Within twenty minutes, the dunes dissolve into a shallow, mile-long lake, knee-deep, brackish, backed by the spongy bog I'd seen from the plane. Shorebirds storm the sky—western sandpipers, plovers, dowitchers, and others whistle overhead in great flocks, jinking as single-minded masses. Sandhill cranes meander, circling and gliding high above, calling with cracking voices. Tundra swans honk, and geese of all kinds yelp in north-bound gangs. From the bog, a stench that is rich, repulsive, sulfuric, stains the air; pintails, wigeons, shovelers, and teal in flocks of hundreds roar out of the stinking grass. The hiking now is slow, each step uncertain, painful for soft, winter-fat thighs.

⸺

This is what steelhead do to me. They send me out in the rankest weather of spring and fall, searching. They have become something of an obsession, an addiction, and like any junkie, I'm at a loss to explain exactly why. The appeal is complex—everything that draws me to flyfishing can be found in chasing steelhead.

Here's how it begins. I fish because something inside says I have to, it is a basic instinct, an impulse as natural and true as the rising sun. I am drawn as a hunter by the stalk, the study, the questions, the possibility of success. The reward occurs when all of these merge into one electric instant and the rod comes alive and the line screams off my reel as a desperate creature struggles insanely against me.

(A confession: late at night, when I'm on my back and my body's stopped twitching, I dream of these moments. Sometimes, after the take, a monster fish drags me into a swift, frothing river, and I awaken with a start.)

Beyond these commonalities, steelhead stand apart. They are big and powerful, like salmon, but not as common; they do not come in perfectly-minted, mass-produced droves to spawn once and die in rotting stacks. Instead, each fish is an individual, distinguished by color, size, and form, a struggling sliver of wildness and light.

Steelhead lead me to places that agree with my nature, to streams that are remote, unpolluted, unpeopled. I have not mastered these sea-run trout and am often baffled by their fickleness. I find them holding in the shadows of runs flowing deep and cool, but there's never a guarantee that I'll get one to strike. When I do hook one and pull it from the river, when I grip its writhing coldness, meet its iron glare, touch its metallic flanks, I feel the junkie's rush, euphoric, undeniable. I have counted coup, and all the work and misery of wind and rain, the many fishless hours, are compensated by a spiritual fullness. But in the end it's only a fix. The craving always returns.

Two hours later I'm still marching, in a driven drizzle, among tussocks and seeps, grass to my armpits. Steller's jays, cobalt tails melding like winter nights into black, crested heads, scream in the brush. I pause for a moment to find my bearings. I can't tell whether the trickles tracing my forehead and cheeks are products of rain or strain. My heart pounds. Close by, on the far side of a thicket, the river whispers.

For a moment, there among the sobbing alders, the questions gnaw. What if I've come all this way for nothing? What if the steelhead are not here, have never been here? Yet hope is at the heart of this sport, where each cast is a question, a defiant probing for truth. Besides, here in the maw of Alaska's coastal wilderness, there's no turning back.

In a heartbeat I am at the river's edge, unaware of the rain, focused on those tannic waters flowing through winter-killed grass and black alder. The stream runs two lanes wide, slow and smooth. The bottom is gravel, scalloped with deep convolutions that make wading tricky. A glare glazes the surface, leaving the water opaque and complicating things further; I might be casting into a pool eight-feet deep or onto a fishless, heel-deep bar.

On a whim, I've passed over the Purple Perils, Skykomish Sunrises, and Skunks, the dressings of tradition. Instead, I've chosen a "Green Screamer," my own name for something new and slightly grotesque: a rabbit-fur strip dyed the color of spring shoots wound over a weighted streamer hook. It is a popular choice for king salmon fresh from the sea, and I figure that the habits of returning sea trout might not be so different from those of salmon. I have, however, downsized the pattern from king-sized #3/0 to #6. Anyway, the whole point of this trip is to crack mysteries and break molds. In a moment, I am casting.

Steelhead are like lovers, you always remember your first one. Mine came on a dusky September evening that smelled of spruce pitch and Borax-cured salmon roe. I was fishing on the Kasilof River for late-run silver salmon—meat-fish for the freezer. I recall my shock at the strike, so sudden, explosive, escalating instantly into a frenzied run that ended seconds later with a thirteen-pound trout beaching itself in a wild leap.

I encountered them again one summer on Kodiak Island's Karluk River while casting dry flies with a five-weight in a hatch of green drakes. Mostly I caught Dolly Varden, two, three pounds apiece, but every third or fourth fish turned out to be a steelhead. They weren't mature—one-and-a-half, two pounds— but they *were* steelhead, novelties that lent the episode a unique kick.

After that, a certain intrigue began to evolve. I stalked steelhead on winter visits to Roderick Haig-Brown's Vancouver Island where I found them sulking darkly in the Stamp and Cowichan rivers. I caught them on Alaska's Kenai Peninsula in the famous Anchor River, where they grabbed dark streamers and tore downriver like hooked bulls. Intrigue welled into fever and somewhere along the line, I discovered that I'd grown serious about flyfishing for steelhead. All of which has led to this moment, this curious Gulf Coast quest.

For an hour there are no signs. Just the gentle river simmering in a steady rain, and peeping birds—juncos, sparrows, kinglets, and so many nondescript little brown warblers and whistlers that I can't keep track of them all. Then, at the edge of a drop-off marked by faint riffles, a fish tails. I see the squared caudal cut the surface, wag softly, and, with a forceful sweep, disappear. I cast a streamer above the drop-off and watch it dissolve into the deep water.

The take is slight, dainty, an almost imperceptible contradiction to the current's steady flow. I haul back, drive the hook into something solid. The fish leaps madly once, twice—at least six times—tumbling in the wet air, landing with loud slaps like a heavy, animated plank. There are several downstream runs, and for a moment, I am perfectly bound by the energy to which I am connected by a weight-forward floating line and pulsing graphite rod.

The runs grow finally weaker and my world, once spinning out of control, begins gradually to slow. Sometimes, when a great fish plays out, the feeling is like stepping off a thrill ride; time, frozen in the course of the struggle, resumes suddenly in measurable form. My hands tremble when the fish, a steelhead hen weighing perhaps ten pounds, turns on its side, allowing me to draw it in and pull the hook. I lower her into the current where she hovers briefly, bright as sunshine on polished chrome. The shroud of mystery, so distinct and heavy an hour ago, has slipped silently away. I blink and the fish is gone.

The next three days are spent exploring both the smooth lower river and two or three miles of dashing, hemlock-lined upper section. Each day brings more steelhead: dark bucks to eight, ten pounds, black-spotted and scarlet-shouldered, with hooked kypes and determined glares; and some hens, slightly smaller, colored more like the silver raindrops that hang glittering from my ferrules. Of course, I hook and lose many others, which is par for steelheading.

Beyond the catching, the beauty of it all is in having an entire river of steelhead to myself. It is high-yield, low-impact wilderness fishing for gems, which in the waning days of this century has grown all too rare. How many steelhead streams remain yet undiscovered? I do not know. But I am aware of other rumors, and they are reassuring. They drive my beating heart.

Four days after setting down in the dunes, I'm standing at the window of Steve Ranney's shack, sipping hot cocoa, examining my reflection. The sun has broken out and the clouds have lifted, revealing a massive glacier beyond my river at the foot of the jagged Coastal Range. A dash of iridescent emerald appears on glittering wings, hovers at collar level in the translucent image of my red chamois shirt. My plane is due. The hummingbird vanishes.

And so I'm left wondering here on the eve of my departure whether that river on the far side of the bog might one day be famous, like the Babine in British Columbia or the Kenai Peninsula's Anchor. If so, it will be with no help from me. Through this region flow many rivers. And if, as some have claimed, the essence of fishing is to solve a mystery, or many mysteries, then finding the pristine place, like the proper pattern, forms the center of our purpose.

Deep South

Life, death, and flyfishing for steelhead
in Alaska's pristine Southeast

Evergreen. That's what comes to mind when you step off a 727 in Wrangell and realize that this country is different. Red cedar, western hemlock, shore pine, Sitka spruce—great, towering trees hung with fat moss beards. Each lends its own subtle shade of green, its own scent, all vaguely gin-like, except for the cedar whose fragrance stands apart, tangy in a woody sense, reminiscent of woodshop and handcrafted jewelry boxes.

The blend of color and smell is fresh, distinct, wild; it is the essence of this place, the Panhandle, Alaska's own Deep South.

Southeast Alaska is a place of fjords and temperate rain forest, of wet summers and comparatively mild winters. Annual rainfall averages 100 to 150 inches. Rubber knee-boots are called "Southeast Alaska sneakers" here, and foul-weather gear is considered casual outerwear. Detached from the state's main body by latitude, geography, and a temperate climate, Southeast is often overlooked by all but those who live here, loggers and commercial fishermen mostly, dwellers of cozy, oceanfront villages that smell of creosote pilings and soured fish.

Over the years I've visited the Panhandle only a few times. Once, when my mother lived in Douglas, we trolled for king salmon near Tenekee Springs in her husband's new boat (a twenty-four-foot Bayliner, fire-engine red, that we bought in

Sitka and sailed to Juneau). We caught salmon, saw deer standing on stony beaches, heard the gulls mewing on high, rock-faced rookeries stained white with guano.

And once, a few years back, the visitor's bureau in Ketchikan invited me down from my home in Wasilla to catch more kings and halibut. The day was rough, stained black and gray by rain, wind and clouds. We caught more fish than I can remember, looking up occasionally to see Canada to the south, sulking in the mist.

Now it is the last week in April and, for the first time, I'm visiting Southeast beyond the confines of salt chop and small craft. The floatplane that brought us here is gone, back to Wrangell, and I'm standing on Prince of Wales Island with two friends on a yellow-sand beach, between a USDA Forest Service cabin and a dead-calm lake.

In the exclusiveness intrinsic to islands, Prince of Wales is not easily visited. First you must cross the Inside Passage, an islet-studded saltwater channel that on gentle spring days is serene, like an enormous blue lake. A thirty-minute floatplane hop gets you here from Wrangell or Petersburg or Ketchikan, isolated towns that themselves can be reached only by air or water.

Beyond its beaches, Prince of Wales is typical of Southeast: a composite of irregularly contoured mountains creased by streams, dashing, gurgling, bouncing through every convolution and hung with lakes lingering in ancient, timber-lined cirques. The water is mostly tannic, the result of runoff filtered through the acidic soil of coniferous forests. It is a distinctive yellow-brown, the color of a wolf's eye.

For twenty-five bucks a day, our cabin comes with a skiff that will take us to a steelhead stream that drains the lake. Tony Route is busy fitting the skiff with a three-horse kicker. Roy Corral is nearby, down on one knee, sorting through a bag of camera gear.

It is evening, nearing the end of a precious bluebird day, and the sun is low, the light like gold.

Mayflies flutter over the lake, backlit and glowing, along with a few caddis and lumbering spruce moths. Our rods are laying in the sand, still in their tubes, when a pair of wakes appears offshore below the skiff. Tony and I hustle down to look, but all we can see are two shadows, each the length of a man's forearm, playing grab-ass in the shallows.

"Cutts?" I ask.

"Big cutts," Tony answers, doubtful. "Steelhead, maybe."

But who knows? That's what the rods are for—positive identification.

Twenty minutes later, I've strung a six-weight and am running the skiff up the lake; Roy is perched in the bow, examining the world through a Nikon viewfinder. Tony's stayed behind, distracted by fish rising in the lake near the cabin. I can look back over our wake and see him for quite a distance, standing in the fading evening light, pipe smoldering, casting a home-tied Quill Gordon to those dancing silver rings.

Tony is a hard-bitten flyfisher with New England ties and a deep love of solitude and twelve-year-old scotch. He abandoned Massachusetts for Alaska fifteen years ago, chucking a degree in entomology to work as a freelance writer. Sometimes, when he's releasing a red-bellied Dolly Varden or when he's sitting by a campfire sipping a tin cup of sixty-dollar single malt, he'll mumble something about a rural tract back east where he grew up and the little brook trout he cut his teeth on.

"All built up now," he'll say. Then he'll shake his head. "Too damn many people."

Roy and I have been out for an hour and now it's getting too dark to see. We pull up at the mouth of a narrow inlet stream and see deer tracks in the sand, find where a black bear had grubbed for skunk cabbage. No fish, though. So we're headed back, through the blackness. The spring air, now that the sun's down, has grown cold, threatening frost, and I can't see a thing until we round a point and spot an orange light quivering in the distance. Campfire. Tony's already sitting on the beach below the cabin, puffing his briar, tasting some scotch. I can smell the hemlock burning, salty, with a vague turpentine edge. We'll get there okay. That scotch will melt in our mouths.

⟨⟨⟩⟩

Morning. Not a cloud in the sky, not a breath of wind. Loons call through a veil of mist on the lake's far side. We are blessed. The plan today is to wade the outlet stream, check out the water, see if we can find some steelhead.

Southeast Alaska, isolated and wild, is among the planet's last, best steelhead strongholds. They're found in hundreds of streams here, mostly small runs of 100 or fewer fish. Many streams are narrow and brushy, often difficult to work. That, along with the region's seclusion, keeps the fishing here generally intimate.

By mid-morning, we are in the boat, buzzing along the shoreline toward the creek. The kicker is slow, straining under the weight of three men, but the lake is calm and we have time.

Actually, I've been thinking about time a lot lately, to the extent that I wonder if I'm verging on some sort of mid-life crisis. At age thirty-four, I'm probably a little young for that kind of thing, but this morning, as I knelt over the lakeshore to wash my face, I could see the crow's feet around my eyes. Reminded me of a dream I'd had a few weeks earlier that was so vivid, so incredibly clear, that I still wonder if it wasn't at least partly real. In the dream I was sitting at my desk when I noticed someone standing in the doorway. It was my grandfather, and he was smiling brilliantly. I was so thrilled to see him that I nearly forgot he'd died when I was sixteen years old. I leaped up and hugged him. I'd never seen him so happy. Then he spoke.

I can't remember everything, but I do clearly recall his words, *"The angel is beautiful ..."*

I know it all sounds pretty weird now, but I felt he was reassuring me, letting me know that I've nothing to fear, that death is not so much an end as it is a transition. For a while the dream and its message were comforting. Then I began to worry that it might be a premonition.

I'm pleased to report that my fears were unfounded. But it did make me see that life—*my* life—is finite. Made me realize that there's so much in this world to do and see. Sometimes I wish I could live a thousand lives, all different. I would like to see the world as a soldier, a musician, a cop, an actor ...

For some things, perhaps, it is never too late. But life is a river that flows one way, and already I can hear doors slamming behind me. Fishing, at least, is timeless. As long as I can stand and swing my arms, I can fish. And I will.

The outlet creek drains an open muskeg dammed by beavers, then disappears into a cavern of evergreens. We follow a game trail into the forest, winding among old-growth hemlocks with fifteen-foot bases, along the singing, wolf's-eye waters. Thrushes trill in the shadows, bald eagles scold from a tree-top nest high overhead.

Our first fish is hooked within half an hour, in a hissing bottleneck where the stream hurries through a rocky gap. The strike is a sharp thump against the stiffness of my eight-weight rod. My line tightens suddenly and a cutthroat trout skips over the riffles out front. Perhaps ten inches long, the cutt is no match for a heavy stick built for ten-pound steelhead. Sooner than I'd like, it surrenders on its side, red-slashed gills beaming in the rain forest's muted light.

Roy and Tony have worked downstream. Rufous hummingbirds buzz around my head, infatuated by the red embroidery on my fishing cap. I hook a resident rainbow trout in the next pool, a game, fourteen-inch tough, black-speckled with flanks the color of smoked honey. Again, the struggle is a spark, short but flashing, punctuating a day of rare Southeast sunshine.

I can't help thinking that this is steelhead water in the classic sense, unpeopled, clean, with swift chutes pouring into deep, dark pools, and plenty of boulders, white water, and log jams for cover. Every cast is an invitation; my forearm is cocked for the take, ready for the lightest bump. But for the next hour or so, my invitations are answered only by fly-snagging, stream-bottom rocks.

Steelhead fishing is perhaps twenty percent skill and luck, and eighty percent timing. Steelhead are sea-run rainbow trout, anadromous fish that spawn in freshwater, spending the bulk of their lives at sea. In their habits, steelhead seem to be something of a cross between salmon and trout. Here in Southeast, they may appear in streams to spawn almost any time, though mostly they run in spring or fall.

On Prince of Wales Island, spring-run fish arrive in late April or early May. However, low water conditions can sometimes keep steelhead holding outside stream mouths until a good rain ups water levels and sends fish on their way. They are iron-willed, hard-fighting fish, worth chasing all over southern Alaska. But you've got to be in the right place at the right time, and that always is something of a gamble.

Toward noon, the day has grown hot. My hatband is soaked with sweat and my winter-soft legs have grown rubbery. I could stop for lunch, but the water is too tempting. It has steelhead written all over it. In a run that is particularly attractive, dark riffles plunging into a bottomless hole, I toss a #6 Rajah, tinsel-bodied, pink-hackled, polar-bear-winged streamer, into the fast water and let it drift.

At times like this, when you're fishing alone in a remote, pristine place and the action is slow, it is easy to lose focus and just go through the motions. My thoughts are far away when I feel a tug. I twitch back on my rod, halfheartedly, figuring it is just another rock. What comes back, telegraphed through eight-and-a-half feet of polished graphite, is not a rigid, grating, unmoving weight. This time, the rock pulls back with a soft, surging, familiar heaviness.

I know before the fish starts to run that it is a steelhead and that I have not properly set the hook. There is a sudden rush of adrenaline, I lean back, put the cork to him and, in less time than it takes to tell, the fish is gone.

Later, mid-afternoon, I meet my friends sitting in dappled April light on a flat rock below a waterfall. The place and the moment have merged to define them: Tony, the angler, has hooked and landed two steelhead—small fish, he says, six and eight pounds; Roy, the artist, has forsaken rods and flies for photography. Both seem happy as hell, like me. Southeast Alaska will do that for you. It is a capricious, powerful place of rain and sun, of seaweed, sand, and briny air, of forests bristling with great green trees. It steals into your head and lodges in your heart; it brings out the best in people and once you've been here, you may find that you never want to leave.

Roy's a character. He's in his late forties, has lived in Alaska for more than thirty years, been divorced a couple times. Spend a little time with him, and you'll discover that Roy is a guy who follows his heart. He's traveled the world on a shoestring, worked as a counselor and as a banjo-picking nightclub singer, cracked his head jumping off an Alaska Railroad car near Fairbanks while playing hobo, and lived on a homestead in the middle of the Brooks Range. But his passion is photography, and his pictures of Alaska, its creatures and its moods, are well known.

Right now, Roy's down in the lake, buck-naked, splashing, screaming like a loon. It's the evening of our third day, another sunny, hot one—seventy-six degrees by Roy's portable thermometer. A regional record-breaker. Today we thought we'd relax, sleep in, and visit the creek with our light rods for cutts. But at the last minute, Tony had decided to leave his rod in the boat and just take some pictures, like Roy. I'd shrugged, put on my vest, and picked up my four-weight.

We got started sometime after lunch. The afternoon was pleasant, there in the rain forest's cool shadows. I spent a couple hours casting into pools fronted by moss-covered stones. Fishing, even for small trout, was slow, but I did manage to hook a two-pound Dolly Varden that I knocked on the head to eat for dinner.

The steelhead, we'd discovered over the last two days, were hanging out in a long, deep stretch of "frogwater"—a currentless, slough-like channel that slithered between banks bristling with salmonberry brambles. It was unlikely steelhead water, difficult as hell to fish, but it was the place Tony had hooked two fish the first day.

As it turned out, there weren't many steelhead in the creek to begin with. We'd fished all the way to saltwater, probing every pool, every likely run. But with the exception of the fish I'd lost on the Rajah in that perfect, churning pocket, we'd found just a few in the frogwater. Apparently, low water and sunny skies had conspired against us. The main steelhead run was behind schedule.

We'd stopped to pick fiddlehead ferns for dinner along that

calm, brushy channel when I looked up and saw a long, dark shadow holding in a beam of sunlight. The fish was in a tough spot, and when I stood to make a cast, it slid out of sight, into the deep, dark stuff. I tried a couple of clumsy casts with the four-weight, then walked backed into the trees and offered it to Tony.

Some guys are at their best in difficult situations. Tony's that way. With a graceful cast and confident crouch, he has pulled fish out of the most unlikely places. I handed him my fly box, watched him tie on an ugly, purple Egg-sucking Leech. Then he stepped out well downstream and dropped the fly next to the brushy far bank. I figured it was a lost cause and was starting to open a can of kippers when I looked up and saw Tony holding that little four-weight high over his head. The rod was bowed and twitching and suddenly something big was rolling out front.

The struggle was slow, powerful, deliberate. With that light rod, Tony had no choice but to let the steelhead wear itself out. He followed it carefully, letting it take line when necessary, leading it as a skilled toreador would lead a bull. The fish thrashed once or twice on the surface, showing blood-red flanks and dark olive back, but never jumped. Mostly it just bulldogged deep, the way cohos do after they've passed their prime in freshwater. Still, the fish was big—bigger, Tony said, than his first two—and tough on that four-weight. But in the end, it was like watching Evander Holyfield pound a sluggish George Foreman.

Soon enough, Tony was kneeling in the shallows, reaching into the amber water. The fish he pulled out would have gone twelve pounds, quite large, we suspected, for this particular run.

"Second-spawn fish," Tony said. "Probably his last time around." Unlike Pacific salmon, steelhead can spawn more than once, returning to the ocean to rejuvenate in between. But the odds of survival drop exponentially after the second time.

More fish splashed upstream under overhanging brush. Tony

handed me the rod, offered a couple tips on where to stand and told me to go get 'em. These steelhead were reminding me more of fall cohos all the time, the way they hid out in the deep, still water in the shadows of undercut banks. The fish apparently had been in the stream for some time and were getting territorial prior to spawning.

I walked downstream, clumsily, spooked a steelhead in the shallows that had been basking unseen, then waded across to get into position. I could see Tony and Roy on the far side, snapping pictures, giving me the thumbs-up. I'd stalked within casting range when a fish tailed near the brush. I dropped my Egg-sucking Leech above that spot and waited, tense, like a coiled spring. There was no mistaking the take on that light, sensitive rod. I reefed back, figuring I'd have to make up in muscle for what the four-weight lacked in backbone. There was a heavy, throbbing resistance and then the fish began to run. I shouted and my friends came running, cameras ready. And then, as with the Rajah two days earlier, my line fell suddenly limp. I reeled in and looked at my fly. I'd put off buying hooks until the last minute and had settled for some light wire models. The stouter stuff was out of stock. As a result, my hook had bent out and there was no one to blame but myself.

I fished hard for the rest of day, while Roy and Tony hung around patiently. Never got another strike, though I saw a few more steelhead hovering like unanswered prayers in the slow water. Steelhead fishing is that way. They are fickle fish and sometimes that twenty-percent gap of skill and luck can be frustratingly wide. But I'd twice had a piece of them, and in such a beautiful setting, with such unheard-of weather, that was all I could ask for.

Roy's done with his bath down at the lake and he's stopped hollering and stepped back onto the beach to dry off. I'm sitting on the cabin porch, sipping Tony's scotch, watching the sunset. Way off, echoing over the hills above the lake, I can hear the moan and chatter of a chain saw. Ominous. A few clearcut scars can be seen from the beach, in the distance, creeping in. Reminds me of my concerns about time, ticking away, not only for me, but for this place, its wildness, its steelhead. The scotch burns my mouth, makes my tongue tingle.

Tony's calling from the cabin. He's fried up that Dolly in butter, along with some potatoes and onions and fiddlehead ferns. We've got one more night here, then its back to another reality: the city and traffic, deadlines and exhaust fumes. But for now we're far away, savoring in the solitude a certain sense of security. After dinner, we'll try to make the trip last as long as possible, sitting out on the beach, next to the fire, talking all night under a scintillating display of rare Southeast stars.

Tony's going to throw it out if Roy and I don't get in there and eat. So I'm getting up, thinking there's no place on earth quite like Southeast Alaska in springtime. I wish they'd shut down that damned saw.

The First Fish

Clouds crept in three days ago, black and heavy with rain that poured without stopping until early this morning. That, combined with the headwaters snowmelt of late May, has left Clear Creek turbid and swifter than usual, jumping its gravel banks to wander rogue-like among greening willows and fireweed shoots.

I've walked upstream for nearly a mile, searching for pools, eddies—places where the water might hesitate enough to allow fish to hold. A slough entering the creek's far side offers such a place, but the main channel proves an uncrossable boundary. Arctic terns hover over the slough, dropping abruptly out of the sky, splashing down and coming up with tiny silver fish that flash in the light like jackknife blades. I count at least thirty, more than I can recall ever seeing in one place. And then, amid those frenzied birds, I spot the wakes of rising fish—fish much larger than those wiggling in the red beaks of diving terns. Aha.

Well beyond casting range, I settle in to watch, an amateur detective holding nothing more than a fly rod and a handful of clues. The small fish attracting the terns are likely salmon smolt, young pinks, perhaps, or silvers, born of gravel wombs following a winter's incubation. They will remain in the stream for a year or two, feeding on plankton and insects, gaining size and strength for their transitory lives at sea.

The larger fish are probably grayling, renowned eaters of floating insects. I'm not surprised to see them. Grayling inhabit thousands of wild Alaskan streams, many little more than trick-ling tundra brooks, nameless and remote. They are delicate crea-tures, innocent as the waters they tread, the lion's share passing their days levitating in glass-clear pools where fake bugs of feath-ers and fur never appear.

When I was young, grayling were for me what bluegills often are for kids in the Lower Forty-eight: the first fish, common, generally easy to catch. Starting at age five, wearing rubber break-up boots and a second-hand wool jacket, I spent my Au-gusts along the gravel bars of the Nelchina River country fly-fishing for them while my elders hunted caribou.

The fish that I brought back to camp on forked willow stringers were rolled in pancake flour, fried hissing and popping in bacon grease, and served to hungry hunters. The fried tails, crisp like potato chips, were my favorites.

I caught them on dry flies—Black Gnats, Mosquitoes. Often I fished a Royal Coachman, the ubiquitous dressing of brown hackle, white quill wings, and red-sashed peacock-herl body. The Coachman doesn't really match any hatch, but it looks enough like a wayward bug that grayling rarely let it pass. Hell, far as that goes, I've watched them rise to cottonwood fluff, spruce needles, and twigs … whatever. And so grayling have branded themselves in my memory as indiscriminate opportunists, ready to make a meal of nearly anything the current brings them.

The morning passes slowly in a mile of dashing, off-color water. The few fishable pockets are suited best to weighted streamers dredged along the bottom. It is not the light, artful casting of *flyfishing*, the fashionable, idyllic sport, but a forceful, grinding way to pick up a couple of foot-long, bottom-hugging rainbow trout.

By lunch time, a cottonwood flat thick with fiddlehead ferns offers a welcome distraction. Sautéed in butter and splashed with vinegar, fiddleheads are delicacies with an asparagus-like texture and flavor reminiscent of spinach and pine nuts; they go nicely with a Zinfandel and fresh fish. So in an instant my hat is off, to serve as a container and rough measure of a meal-sized collection.

Salmonids and wild greens taste best in the spring; I almost never kill trout, char, or grayling any other time. Altruism has nothing to do with it. Fact is, I simply do not enjoy eating fish on a regular basis. Yet I'm aroused once or twice a year by the thought of firm, white flesh, steaming hot, seasoned lightly with garlic and lemon, sprinkled with almond slivers browned and crisped in the oven. Wild fern sprouts are a seasonable, natural compliment.

Fiddlehead picking leads me off the creek, but on the far side of the cottonwoods I'm drawn to an opening where a high-water channel flows. The stream here is narrow, slower; you can wade across it. Stepping out of the trees onto a sandy bar, I discover a place where the water piles into a cutbank, forming a deep pool that turns and flows against itself. It is a likely spot, and even as I watch, a fish jumps, suddenly—leaps clear out of the water. Grayling.

I'm studying the pool now, finding many fish rising. I've got them, I'm sure. A dry fly of nearly any kind will have them eating out of my hands. I tie on a Black Gnat, since it is the only floating fly I have; carelessly, I've left my dry-fly box at home.

Of course, the heart of flyfishing lies in solving problems. Observation leads to knowledge, of the prey and of its prey. If you play the game right, your fly becomes a convincing counterfeit link in the food chain. At the moment, a few mayflies flutter overhead on backlit wings. Close to the bank, caddis are hatching. I see nothing over the water that appears to resemble a Black Gnat, though that's not particularly important. I've never known grayling to stop at appearances.

A fish splashes midway in the pool and I measure out line carefully, then cast to the spot. My rod, a long, willowy four-weight, was made for this: a weightless dry fly, light tippet thin as hair. I'm gripping the cork in anticipation, waiting for the imminent strike. Nothing. I cast again, and a grayling flashes a foot away from my bobbing Gnat, snubbing it for God-knows-what.

It is difficult at times like this not to feel betrayed, considering I have hunted these fish since I was four years old. I knew them, I thought, and yet it seems right now that I know nothing at all. Alaska, however, is an enormous sum of countless parts: mountains, glaciers, weather. Fish. Mysteries here have a way of leading to more questions and sometimes it takes something as humble as grayling, the first fish, to remind us that, no matter how much we think we know, we can never have all the answers.

A wake, tiny, struggling, appears on the surface; it makes me wonder. Kneeling, I take my hand and scoop up a salmon smolt the size of a guppy. All at once, everything falls into place—the shrieking terns, the bugless rises ...

The Black Gnat is traded for a tinsel-bodied, bug-eyed streamer I've tied with meat-hungry trout and char in mind. My cast this time is tentative, without presumption, and in a heartbeat, I'm into a pot-bellied grayling as long as my forearm. I feel like cheering, realizing a sense of delight and validation that takes me back to those far-off Nelchina days. I am a little older now, but something within me is warmed to know that over thirty-some years, nothing's really changed.

Arctic grayling are many things: an herbal smell, faint, lingering in the palm; artful studies in pre-Pleistocene biology, as suggested by their unique dorsals, out-sized and arcane. And yes, they are delicate sippers of riparian bugs, surface-feeders, ring-makers. But grayling, more than anything else, are survivors.

When the last ice age a few hundred-thousand years ago glaciated much of Alaska, grayling (along with such other old-timers as lake trout and northern pike) endured in more temperate pockets of the North Slope and in the Yukon River Valley. They spread as the ice melted gradually, distributing themselves over most of mainland Alaska. An ability to survive in waters offering little dissolved oxygen—a situation common in long winters when still, shallow pools sealed beneath thick layers of ice and snow become virtually anaerobic—allows grayling to inhabit places other fish cannot.

Grayling, in one form or another, are circumpolar. (I'm told that several species are found in streams in the Russian Far East, including a large, black version flashing piranha-like teeth.) Haig-Brown caught them in his native Britain, and in North America grayling once were common as far south as Michigan. The usual culprits—habitat loss, overfishing, and competition from introduced species—wiped grayling out of most of their Lower Forty-eight range, proving that as tough as they are in terms of nature, the ring-makers really are as delicate as they appear in the hands of man.

The gaudy, flaglike dorsal, the grayling's defining appendage, is distinct but abstruse. Membranous and marked with pink and powder-blue spots, its main function may be for display and intimidation in rituals held near spawning beds. Grayling are covered with iridescent scales that appear silver, turquoise, and purple in a metallic sort of way. White bellies are framed by stripes the color of gold dust.

An eye for opportunity and diversity is the species' secret to success in unforgiving environments. On windless August evenings, tundra lakes often boil with the rings of grayling feeding on swarming midges, caddis, and mosquitoes. In streams where salmon congregate to spawn, the ring-makers become egg-suckers, greedily choking down protein-rich salmon eggs. Seven months later, when hatching salmon wriggle free of natal gravel, grayling are there to greet them. Larger grayling sometimes grab and eat water shrews and voles, which may sound a little desperate until you consider that Alaska, more perhaps than anywhere else, is a land of feast or famine. When dinner's served, fish here usually eat—no questions asked.

Even so, growing seasons in Alaska remain short and grayling mature slowly. An eleven-inch fish, ready to spawn for the first time, may be five years old or older. Grayling are generally petite; fourteen-inchers are considered by most to be better than average; sixteen- to eighteen-inch fish are hogs. The state record, caught in the early 1980s, spanned twenty-three inches and weighed a girthy 4 lbs. 13 oz.

Grayling are spring spawners, returning en masse when rivers and lakes thaw, to common spawning gravel. A month or so later, they migrate to feeding areas in headwaters—often shallow, rocky, mountain and tundra streams flanked by willow and sedge. Fry, meanwhile, begin to hatch following three weeks of incubation. The young fish remain nearby for the summer, in slower waters. Finally, when the willows turn yellow with autumn's first frosts and shelf ice appears on headwater streams, adult grayling turn tail and migrate down to major rivers where they winter in deep channels unlikely to freeze solid.

Canoe Lake. May seventh. My good friend Greg-the-Cop is leaning back in his float tube, ranting about department politics (a sergeant's position is up for grabs and the squad room seems to be getting cutthroat) when a fish boils in the shallows. Greg stops mid-sentence, his cop Raybans locked mechanically on the dissipating ring, calibrating like a radar gun.

The morning is cold, the predawn ether hard, edgy. This is wool-glove season; a skin of overnight ice clings to shoreline sedges. My breath is coming in frosty gray puffs, and I am watching Pioneer Peak silhouetted in the east, wondering if I can wait much longer for the sun to top the summit.

Greg is casting now, pushing aside his troubles to plop an olive-and-black Lake Leech into the center of the rise. He hesitates, then reefs his rod tip high. No head-shaking leaps or line-peeling dashes follow. Just a pleasurable, throbbing sequence of subsurface runs that start out strong, but fade too soon into a long, waving dorsal breaking the water like a flag of surrender.

Tubing this weedy, shallow lake west of Palmer, an old farm-colony town of strikingly midwestern grid and 1950s architecture, has become part of a spring rite for Greg and me. The fish all are grayling, mulling the shoreline in huge spawning schools, and if you catch one this time of year, you will likely catch thirty—or sixty, depending mostly upon your tolerance for numb fingers and cold feet.

Actually, the scores of lakes in this part of Alaska—the Matanuska and Susitna valleys—have earned a reputation among flyfishers for fine spring trout fishing. Trouble is, this early in May, many are still covered with rotting ice. Those that are ice-free have yet to turn over (that mysterious phenomenon where temperature layers flip-flop under the warming sun, stirring warmth and oxygen into the cold blood of trout gone lethargic in the icewater of winter). But Canoe Lake, shallow, fixed like a hinge in the path of a wandering sun, is among the first area lakes to open each spring. It is close to home and while the rainbow fishing remains dead, the grayling are eager.

The catching improves as sunlight sprays over Pioneer Peak. We're into a pod of spawners and have rediscovered, as we do each spring, that the best way to hook them is to let our weighted streamers sink for a ten-count, then twitch them in with short, electric strips. At one point, we're both playing fish simultaneously, and Greg leans over and says this is too much fun and that we really should try to get together a little more often. We're both laughing, giddy, the winter blues breaking up like ice in a mild spring breeze.

I'm into a fish that is struggling, tugging with all of its sixteen-inch might, when I glance at Greg and see him reaching into the lake, pulling out a grayling, fat, glittering, gasping in the yellow morning light. For the moment, my friend is no longer pistol-packing, squad-car-driving Greg-the-Cop, six-foot-one, 200 brawny, hairy-knuckled pounds. He is the same kid with whom I fished twenty-two years ago, and nearly every year since, worry-free, an unlikely poet with a heavyweight punch and the gentle heart of a priest. An old man once told me that, over the course of a lifetime, you can count such friends on the fingers of one hand.

The morning passes. Greg has just released another fish, his twentieth or, maybe, twenty-fifth, and is glancing at his watch, shaking his head. He's pulled an afternoon shift. There are thieves to catch, speeders to stop. The spell, suddenly, is broken. Life again grows serious.

We're back at the parking lot where we met at dawn, putting away our waders and rods, climbing into our trucks. Greg is not happy leaving when the fishing's so good; it pains him, you can see it in his face. Not so many years ago, before life became so resolute, he would have stayed, played hooky. But we've traveled too far in a short time.

I have the day off; this is my weekend. I'm thinking I will head back to the house and warm up with eggs over-easy and a steaming cup of tea. Then I'll return to the lake, to spring and the hungry fish. But it won't be quite the same without Greg. Nothing in Alaska or anywhere else is quite like the company of good, old friends. But those grayling and I go back a long way.

Breakup at Shady Lake

Everyone wants revenge,
but scarcely anyone does anything about it.
—Jim Harrison

When I arrived at Shady Lake, the last snow patches had dissolved in May's mild breezes and winter was but a dark, cold memory. As I threaded steel leader through a heavy graphite fly rod, sensations of hope and deliverance mingled with murky overtones of revenge.

The working person does not survive an Alaska winter without bruises. I was coming off a particularly brutal period of long, snow-blown commutes and too many hours spent holed up in an office. The usual periods of tension and cabin fever could have been averted by getting out more, but somehow I had endured. Now I was standing shin-deep in sedges, toying with the long-held notion that sometimes the best revenge in life is simply to live well. And for the moment, that meant fishing. Lots of fishing.

The Susitna Valley is full of lakes like Shady—black, tannic cauldrons that bubble with sulfuric gases, the product of decaying swamp plants and nondescript biota. These are sullen, gloomy places, haunted by creatures with expressionless, robotic eyes and murderous reflexes. I'd seen them in Shady before, cruising the shorelines, cutting wakes among the lily pads where muskrats and ducklings paddled.

I'm talking northern pike. Fish to twenty-five pounds or more. Perfect prey for a frostbitten flyfisher ready to step into the light and shout: *I am alive!*

My flies are wicked as the fish themselves—bright-yellow and blood-red streamers tied on #3/0 hooks; heavy, galvanized-steel shanks long as a man's index finger. They're called "Sea-Ducers," sanguine combinations of rage, fear, and vulnerability. Literally, they imitate nothing. But in an impressionistic sort of way, they seem to inspire everything that is evil and angry in big northern pike.

I'm rigged and ready. Finally. A sourness accumulated over a winter of nervous lethargy is lifting, and for the first time in too many months, I can divine a sense of purpose. The day, the lake, and the pike are all mine, and somewhere in the back of my mind, I can see an old black-and-white television set throbbing with light and can hear Jackie Gleason roaring, "How sweeeeet it is!"

A northern pike's lair is a brew of shadow, cover, and opportunity. The fish hang out in drowned timber and among lily-pad gardens where they can blend in and ambush passing prey—sticklebacks, young trout and salmon, leeches, small mammals, and swimming birds. Even other pike. Their eyes are set high on their heads over long, duck-bill snouts fitted with ragged, flesh-shredding teeth. In that sense they resemble alligators, vaguely reptilian in design, programmed by nature to lunge and kill with sociopathic coldness.

I'm stalking the spongy muskeg shoreline, probing the shallows for dark, serpentine profiles, when a blur at my feet launches into the lake with a splash. Something in my chest leaps and, for an instant, I'm left startled and confused. Then, within casting distance, a black, spear-headed bird necks out of the water, howling. Loon. Thank God. At my feet I discover a bowl-shaped depression of matted grass and sooty down wrapped around two speckled, olive-colored eggs. The seeds of a new beginning, they shed a beam of light upon the moment.

The expectant mother is growing hysterical and I can feel my cheeks blushing like those of a naughty child. There's nothing to do but sidestep the area and hunt elsewhere.

Springtime in Alaska is like that. No matter how many seasons you see, spring here always comes as an abrupt, happy surprise. One minute you're snow-bound in perpetual darkness, the next you're squinting in the sunlight, gripping a fly rod, feeling reborn. It is enough to leave a big, strong flyfisher suddenly weak-kneed and giddy.

Soon I'm in another cove, searching. No pike shapes are visible, the water's too dark for that. Too deep, too many lily pads. It's exactly the kind of place I'm looking for.

In a heartbeat I'm casting, whipping winter's residue out of every joint and muscle. It is a cathartic feeling, like leaping out of a plane and feeling the wind in your face. I could scream.

My streamer hits the water in a gap between the lily pads. Now I must wait, let the fly settle into the cold shadows. Then I strip it in with short, quick pulls.

The take is sudden and violent, bone-jarring. Black water boils like an evil soup and my reel shrieks. Instantly, the fish is pulling my heart out, the way a big pike will on the initial run, and I can feel the new season pulsing in my rod, thumping in my chest. It's all hanging out now, the oppressive darkness and seclusion of more than thirty winters exorcised in a single, desperate surge.

The first run is the best, since pike are sprinters, built not for the long haul, but for that one deadly lunge. And sooner than I'd like, the ride is over; the fish turns on its side, shaking its malevolent head weakly as I reach out and grab a gill.

My emotions now are mellowing in the wake of the struggle, as I hold in my arms this slimy, writhing, twelve-pound symbol of spring. Oddly, in its helplessness, I recognize a veiled innocence beyond those lidless eyes. A voice in my head whispers, *This isn't evil, it's just nature, following the rules, filling a niche.* The fish thrashes as I pull the hook, raking my hand before slipping back into the stinking, swampy water. In a green-backed, white-bellied flash, it is gone.

A stream of blood drips off my index finger into the water and I'm vaguely aware of a long, stinging gash. It is enough to remind me that I have survived another winter and that, for the moment, I'm living well. The frost within has thawed, finally. This is my revenge. *How sweeeeet it is!*

The Season of
Trout Dancing

A dorsal cuts shark-like through the shallows. I'm watching from deeper water, twenty, thirty feet out, stripping line from my reel in careful arm lengths, measuring in my mind the distance of my first cast. High overhead, almost out of sight, a dive-bombing snipe winnows on fluttering wings. *Woo-woo-woo.* It is an eerie, high-pitched progression that accelerates as the bird falls toward earth. From my float tube the air smells like rain-soaked loam, earthy and sweet. Distinctly riparian.

In May, you *hunt* for lake-bound trout, policing shoreline shoals, ankle-deep, gravel-bottomed, for swirls or shimmers that suggest force and mass below. This is the season of trout dancing, when lake rainbows gather to writhe like dervishes, horny and malevolent in the shallows. Unfortunately, in Alaska's land-locked lakes, running water is needed to oxygenate spawn and assure a hatch. So the rituals of the season might appear overtly hollow—like recreational sex at its most basic level. Yet, in the scheme of the times, the driven twisting and chasing seems as rich and meaningful as the budding of birches and the courting of snipe.

Life this time of year radiates from above in the face of an omnipresent sun. The air grows temperate, dissolving snow and ice, leaving puddles that tremor with burping wood frogs. Geese and cranes return in yelping flocks to skies that six weeks earlier were pale and cold, lifeless, save for the shining black silhouettes of ravens. Still, spring remains vaguely out of reach; winter, it seems, can truly die only in the wake of a fat trout hooked in the chill waters of a Susitna Valley lake.

I was introduced to lakes and tubes long ago through a friend who has drifted away with the years. That first night lingers. It was not spring, but coming on fall, late August, when the air grows cool and tangy with the smell of cranberries fermenting. From our float tubes, we worked purple leeches in the shallows under overhanging alders and among breaching snags, and we caught rainbows, beneath the stars, from twelve to sixteen inches long.

That night remains a common denominator behind every shoreline cast and the primary impetus for a special fly I've "invented" and continue to use with great confidence. Really, my "Hybrid" is a modification of the popular Marabou Lake Leech we fished that first night. I've since gone from purple to olive marabou and have simply added black saddle hackle, palmered Woolly-Bugger-style, the length of the body. It imitates everything from dragonfly nymphs to common leeches. From May to October, it is deadly.

For those who don't know them, lakes can appear intimidating, deceptive. I once thought of them as the antithesis of streams: terrestrial prisoners, enormous organic tubs, predictable, boring. But I know them better now and am no longer fooled. Lakes, I've discovered, are fickle as the seasons, cyclical riddles complex as water temperatures and damselfly naiads, testosterone and estrogen, anglers and common loons. Lakes are, in fact, living bodies that pulse and change within. They demand time and careful study.

My lake this evening is without other anglers, as it always is this time of year. There are reasons for this. For one, flyfishing's appeal seems linked, perhaps irrevocably, to the energy and variances of current. Streams have agendas; they're going somewhere and so—the rationale follows as we drift our lines over them—are we.

Too, runs and pools, seams and riffles are icons of tradition. A river runs through the literature of our sport, and Alaska is famous for great rivers. They course the country like veins, serving as highways for men and for fish, fed by the land and promising something in return. When spring arrives, salmon follow and streams within 200 miles of home grow crowded with guides and sports, jet boats and float planes. The atmosphere can be carnivalesque, the attitude being: *Bigger is better* and *Every man for himself.* Local rivers this time of year are not for introverts.

Lakes, meanwhile, promise contrast, something against which to measure things that hustle and chatter. Here, where waters rest and brood, life slows, visions clear; like fog in the light of a rising sun, tensions vanish in the solitude of sedges and white-trunked birches.

Anyway, it is May, and I'm alone, an indulgence I've come to count on, since solitude for me, as much as the catching and fighting and releasing of trout, is what fishing and Alaska are all about.

I'm falsecasting now, finding my range—it's been a long winter and I'm a little rusty. More than a dozen dorsal silhouettes whirl out front, and when everything feels right, I let my fly fall, as delicately as a weighted #8 Lake Leech will, directly into the center of the orgy.

Time now to count: one-one-thousand, two-one-thousand, three ... *the fly must sink to their level.* Now, strip. Pause. Strip again. Pow! I feel the force against my wrist, a heavy, surging, electric resistance. Then things get crazy. The fish bolts, green floating fly line splits the shallows. Abruptly, I'm hanging on as three pounds of solid energy hangs in the air, framed by a halo of sunlit mist, before crashing down with a slap. Synapses crackle and, in the back of my mind, I recognize a catharsis that is sudden and strong—a mysterious, euphoric rush.

In early summer—June here in southcentral Alaska—the lakes continue to offer rainbows, by then bull-headed, snaky caricatures of their pre-spawning selves, spawned-out and spent. Warming water temperatures and longer days send them from the shallows into deep water, broom-tailed and weary, to sulk, feed, and recover. A guy can catch and release a few by using sinking lines rigged with dragonfly nymphs, Zonkers, and Marabou Lake Leeches, though due to the lustful rigors of previous weeks, the warriors of spring have little pep. For a time, I generally leave them alone.

In July and early August, the trout remain deep by day. But at night, as surface temperatures cool, they return to the shallows where mayflies and midges swarm. Casting dry flies (#14 Adams and Blue-winged Olives) or soft hackles (#12 Partridge-and-Yellows tied from spruce grouse capes) in the dusky evening hours provides an exciting twist. This can continue through September, until one morning in October, perhaps while you're off shooting mallards in an early snowstorm, the lake freezes over.

Before I go on, I have an admission to make, one that may provoke surprise or, perhaps, prejudice. Many, though by no means all, of these trout that run and jump, as rainbows will, with impressive stamina and strength, are not native. (Neither, by the way, are most Alaskans.) But when you're manhandling a four-pound rainbow trout damn near as wide as a canoe paddle in a remote Alaska lake, it is difficult to express clearly anything unnatural about them. Such fish—and there are plenty of them—have likely lived in the wild for several years. Emanating shades of burnished honey-brown (to match the tannin water), they are as feral in character, strength, and color as any creature or plant out there.

Yet these fish *are* different. In many cases, their chromosomes have been manipulated to create novel piscatorial entities that biologists call "triploids."

If the vernacular seems foreign—"triploid" and "chromosome manipulation" do have a certain sci-fi ring—think of these manmade fish simply as *designer trout*. After all, the thousands of triploid rainbows swirling in scores of Alaskan lakes have been designed by biologists to keep things simple.

The advantage is this: triploids are sterile and may be placed in locations where trout capable of reproduction are best not introduced. This prevents unnatural genetic mixing in drainages where native trout may be present.

To create sterile triploid trout, fertilized eggs are heat-shocked—soaked during a critical phase of development in water heated to twenty-six degrees C, about 79 degrees F. The warm water breaks down proteins essential for cell division in the eggs, leaving young fish with three sets of chromosomes: two sets from the female and one from the male. As a result, these fish are unable to reproduce, unlike normal trout, called diploids, that have only two sets of chromosomes, one set from each parent.

The triploiding process produces sterile trout *nearly* 100 percent of the time—the state Broodstock Center at Fort Richardson near Anchorage averages about 98.5 percent. That's an excellent standard, but close doesn't count in the fish-stocking game. So the process is taken one step farther: hatchery personnel create all-female triploids.

To do this, the sex of normal females is reversed by feeding young trout a hormone—17-alpha-methyl-testosterone—that transforms them all into functional males. Genetically, however, the fish remain females. So when they create sperm cells, the sperm contains only the X (female) chromosome. Sperm from the sex-reversed females is then used to fertilize eggs, and the progeny are all then female.

All of this genetic wrangling is confusing, of course, and labor-intensive. Biologists, therefore, prefer to stock less expensively produced diploid rainbow trout where conditions permit (usually in landlocked lakes unlikely to flood into adjacent drainages). But stocking trout in a fish-crazy place one-third the size of the contiguous forty-eight states is a big job. In 1995, the Broodstock Center produced more than 800,000 fish—rainbow trout, grayling, salmon—to be dumped in selected waters from Ketchikan to Fairbanks.

The hour is late and I'm still hanging in my float tube hunting springtime trout on that wild lake. The water has fallen still and dark as jade, and my only companions are a pair of red-eyed arctic loons, a bald eagle slouching in a cottonwood tree, and dozens of spawning trout. The air temperature, now that the sun has sunk below the birch-fringed skyline, is falling, growing crisp, like September. It is an edgy, magical time.

I'm in the middle of another pod of roiling spawners. I can see them dashing back and forth near the shoreline in a ten-foot circle, creating noisy wakes.

I'd hooked a large fish on my first cast of the evening, but lost it in a heartbeat when it leaped, shaking its head. A couple of casts later, in the same foot or two of water, another trout struck. That one ran and tugged and shook its head, but didn't jump.

The fish was powerful, showing the startling reserve of pure rainbow trout without the additional power of a current. We'd struggled for five full minutes, which out in a tube on a quiet evening seems a good long time, before I netted what turned out to be a purple-sided, hook-jawed buck. The trout was solid, heavy. Better than four pounds, approaching five. I measured the fish against the scale printed on my float tube apron: twenty-two inches.

That was two hours and several fish ago. Now a pale moon shines weakly against a dusky midnight sky, and I'm taking it easy, thinking about how the world from a float tube flows as a collection of vignettes, three-dimensional, ever-running, always changing. Earlier in the evening I'd watched grebes run on water, courting. And in the past I've seen mink and short-tailed weasels bouncing along shorelines, rattling in the dry leaves and grass, disappearing into folds of earth to pop up again atop knotty logs. I've known loons to come to the sounds of hooked trout splashing, eager to pounce on spent fish freshly released. There have been many muskrats, beavers, and ducks.

And once, on a cloudy evening last June, I'd watched a lady flyfisher, blonde, early-thirties, casting alone from a Buck's Bag in the shallows of one of my favorite lakes. She'd pulled in shortly after I'd arrived, driving a dusty '80s-model Ford pickup, and I'd watched furtively when she stepped out and slipped her hourglass body into brown neoprene waders. Her manner and dress were unaffected. There were no cute, fashionable mauves or teals; her float tube was seasoned and stained. The fact that she had come alone suggested an intriguing genuineness. We exchanged silent nods.

On the lake, she cast confidently, smoothly. Her devotion to fishing was clear and, not surprisingly, I was struck by her right away—by her aura of uncommon independence, and by the yellow hair that hung to her shoulders, slack and long. We fished off opposite shores until the sun ducked behind the trees and the light grew smoky. Then she stepped ashore and vanished, her float tube over one shoulder, into the forest near the trailhead.

I don't know exactly what of all of this means, other than perhaps there are no limits, short of winter, to flyfishing in Alaska. It's a big world up here, with plenty of water and fish. It is a place where a man—or a woman—can gear up after work and slip into a dead-calm lake without a word. Or a worry.

Anyway, I'm stepping out of the lake now, ducklike, ready to fall headfirst as I pull off my fins. The trout still are dancing, you can hear them, though the rhythm is winding down as the water cools for the night. Seasons here arrive and pass and, in the end, I am all for that. The trick, as with the trout, is in letting each one go. And moving onto the next.

Summer

Discovering
South Fork

A few bugs are showing as I step out of my truck, spring mosquitoes mostly, big (#10s in the calibrating vernacular of flyfishing), slow, easy to slap. Spears of new grass poke through last year's straw and the evening air is cool, musky with the rot of last fall's leaves. Yet even as spring edges toward summer, my heart tells me that the first week of June is too early for South Fork. Far up in the Talkeetna Mountains, melting snowdrifts have likely turned Susitna Valley streams into furious brown rogues.

Still, here I am, parked at the end of a grown-over road, slipping into my vest, preparing to hike along a moose trail to a run on the river that is short and full of memories and big—I'm talking *heavy*—rainbow trout.

Flyfishers seem drawn to waters that reflect something of themselves, explaining perhaps the sport's diversity of personalities: steelhead fanatics, dry-fly purists, bonefish fools. ... Bound by nature to recreate ourselves in our passions, we return to the places that have shaped us; these are our home waters. And so I am drawn to South Fork, a lonely, moody, overtly humble stream that is handy, yet isolated, promising inspiration without interruption, a place that will not be found listed in the *Alaska Atlas and Gazetteer*—at least, not under that heading.

Of more than thirty accessible stream miles, I fish just two South Fork runs. Today I'm visiting the "lower run," a brief stretch of water scarcely a hundred yards long. Roughly two-lanes wide and swift enough in places to knock you down, the lower run is a composite of pools, riffles, rapids, undercut banks, boulders, and logs; it is a trout magnet, a compact, convoluted reach where you can fish all morning and still not properly cover all the good water.

In a moment my waders are on, five mils of spongy neoprene stretched from toes to chest. Body condom. Canvas vest hangs from my shoulders, ratty and worn, offering a heft that is familiar, satisfying. I'll go ahead and tie on a fly here, a heavy, hairy leech fashioned from rabbit hide and fuse wire wrapped on a #4 streamer hook, the traditional tempter for June on South Fork.

A dozen heartbeats, one angler's knot, and then I'm in gear, walking in felt-bottomed wading boots over those damp, rotting leaves. Secrets of the past lurk in the evening sun's silk-veiled light; I'm reminded now of this place as I first found it years ago, of the accidents that led me here.

A friend, Trevor McReynolds, a globe-surfing, hitchhiking, pony-tailed Canadian, is passing through Alaska, after completing a foot tour of Europe and Russia. He appears one evening in late June, to visit, and—surprise!—to fish. I'm packed for a float trip scheduled for the day after tomorrow. No time for long hikes, camping, or arranging bush flights; our options are limited to the immediate road system. That night as we sip beer and talk, I slip a box of flies from my duffel, figuring we can share the one fly rod I haven't packed, a spare five-weight.

Next afternoon, we pull off at a stream selected at random, work up from a campground packed with motor homes, kids on bicycles, and overflowing dumpsters. This is not, I promise Trevor, Alaska in its classic sense, but it's the best I can provide on short notice.

We're wading wet in water so cold my thighs go numb. (Trevor has no waders, so out of courtesy, I've come without mine.) We drop a Bitch Creek into every pool and pocket. No trout. No grayling. Nothing. Still, we continue, driven.

Upstream, a mile or so beyond the campground, monofilament tangles and boot prints fade, replaced by moose tracks in clean gravel and, in some mud, the dainty, rose-blossom prints of mink. Log jams form deep pools, and undercuts hunker beneath hanks of tall grass. Open bars scattered here and there allow for decent backcasts, and the air is fragrant with the resins of spruce and willow. It smells like gin.

In a fast, neck-deep eddy that I will one day recognize as the foot of my lower run, a pair of ruddy shadows wave in the current. King salmon. Trevor is intrigued; these are the biggest fish he's ever seen. Salmon are a good sign, but a hopeless cynicism has taken root. Absent-mindedly casting and talking, I plop a new fly—a black rabbit-fur Bunny Bug—into a pocket behind the salmon. The strike is instantaneous, fierce, as if I've hit a live wire, and it damn near yanks the rod from my hand. I start to pass the five-weight to Trevor, to be a good host, when I realize that the fish, tearing straight downstream, is a rainbow trout, a solid twenty-inches worth, at least. I'm shouting over the current to Trevor that he can have the next one when, as through an act of karmic retribution, the fish jumps and the hook pulls free.

For a moment, there is nothing in the world but flaccid leader and chattering water. Then, recovering, I turn to Trevor and he grins back wickedly: South Fork holds some by-God *good* rainbow trout.

In late June, solstice time, night's presence in southcentral Alaska is less literal than implied. Sometime around midnight a gradual duskiness settles in; the birds grow quieter, streams run a little louder. Trevor and I cast late into the evening, trading the rod back and forth, each landing and losing several hefty rainbows. For a long while there is nothing to keep us from fishing through

the half-light into the next morning, until abruptly we find ourselves cut off at the junction of a deep, grass-lined beaver slough.

Standing there on the edge, we're both disappointed on one
hand that the fishing is pretty much over, but relieved, too, since
we haven't eaten all day. Besides, it's the time of night when bears
prowl. In front of us, visible in the slough's dark water, a group of
reddish shapes frame a flooded willow snag. I'm pointing out the
salmon to Trevor when another shape, black and as long as my
arm, slides snakelike from under the snag.

The trout is holding just off the bank; there's no need to cast,
which is fortunate, since suddenly I've lost my breath and my legs
are trembling. All I need to do is strip some line, poke out my rod
tip, and lower my leech pattern slowly into the pool.

There is beauty in the action of a rabbit-fur strip in water: it
pulses, contracts, expands. It is art imitating life, stimulus inviting
response. It's in the water now and the long black shape freezes
immediately, becomes rigid. The fuse is lit.

All anticipation is lost to the boiling attack. There is no time, no
real need, to set the hook. Salmon scatter as fly line rips down the
slough for the fast water. Holding on with both hands, I try palm-
ing the reel gently, hoping to slow things down. But just short of
the current, the trout jumps clear. For an instant, it hangs frozen in
mid-leap—a subliminally phallic length of brass-eyed energy—before falling in slow motion, as the great ones always do, back into
the slough with a startling slap. My five-pound tippet snaps like
silk.

Trout like that have a way of putting an evening, and all previ-
ously caught fish, into perspective. Trevor and I stare for a moment into the gloomy water, speechless, unbelieving. Then, tenta-
tively, I wonder aloud if that fish might have gone twenty-five
inches. Trevor shakes his head. No. Twenty-eight, probably better.
(I'm thinking: *Yeah, that's more like it.*)

Later, when we step into the truck, tired, hungry, still in shock,
I ask Trevor, as politely as I can, to forget the creek's real name.

Hell, he says, he may never visit Alaska again. But you can tell he would like to, and that he understands.

Weeks after Trevor and I discovered South Fork, I returned with my most trusted friend, Greg-the-Cop, the patrolman with whom I've fished and hunted since we were both twelve years old. Recently divorced, Greg was drained emotionally and needed what I knew already South Fork had to offer: peace, solitude, and some damned fine trout fishing.

We arrived early, in that misty fringe between night and morning, partly because Greg's dreams were haunted and he could not sleep. The air was still, broken only by the stream's sizzling current. Grizzly tracks blundered across a sandbar on the far bank, causing me to glance over my shoulder now and then. The enormous trout I had lost earlier, though likely an anomaly, had already found its place in legend and as we waded in I retold the story. Greg said nothing, just allowed a respectful measure of silence before changing the subject.

"Ever catch any grayling here?" he asked.

"No," I answered. "Never."

Seconds later we were fishing, and I drifted a Glo-bug through a shady pool and set the hook into a grayling seventeen inches long with scales that flashed like gaudy sequins, turquoise and purple. Greg-the-Cop, unusually quiet, hardly noticed.

More king salmon than ever gathered to spawn in the run. Below them, furtively, in riffles and behind gray stones, rainbows waited, and we had a grand time fooling them with Glo-bugs. At one point, I hollered as I leaned into a struggling trout, but Greg, releasing the only Dolly Varden I have seen caught in South Fork to this day, could not be bothered. He seemed far away, in a sort of trance. I watched for a moment as he held the dripping, sparkling fish gently, then lowered his hands and looked at the water, seeing, I guessed, an image of himself and no one else. I imagined he was sorting things out, rediscovering, perhaps, precisely who he was. Good fishing can do that.

Anyway, Greg seemed happier after that, and for a couple hours we continued catching fish. There were several nice rainbows—some just a shade under twenty inches and three pounds—but no monsters.

I'd fished downstream, almost to the end of the run, when I noticed several spawned-out kings scattered along a gravel bar. Gulls had plucked out the eyes, adding a ghastly touch to the already grimacing, decaying carcasses. As I crunched across the gravel, I noticed one of those kings seemed oddly darker in color and I caught myself wondering.

Kneeling closer I saw the black-speckled olive head, rose-blushed gill plate. Birds had peeled back the skin and eaten much of the flesh, but the backbone and tail remained intact. In the spirit of a classic novel concerning a man and a great billfish, I picked up the carcass. I walked downstream and found Greg fishing a little riffle. When I held up the dead rainbow, his face turned white.

"Thirty inches?" he asked. "Thirty-two?"

I just shook my head, figuring maybe Freud was right when he said there are no accidents. At that moment, South Fork's legend not only lived on, it grew. I looked over my shoulder and tossed the evidence into the current.

"Damn, that was a big rainbow," Greg-the-Cop whispered, as we walked back to the truck.

"Forget it," I answered.

Length alone, by the way, is not an accurate measure of South Fork trout. These fish are elliptical, bloated, girthy, like piscine blimps. They also are unusually solid and powerful. A two- or three-pound rainbow hooked at the top of the run is guaranteed to turn tail and scream downstream through a short stretch of rapids I call the Rock Garden. If, like me, you're into fishing light tackle on small streams, you'll skip down the gravel bar after that fish. If the fish isn't too big, the battle usually ends in a tapering tug of war where the fast water piles into a pool formed by a natural driftwood dam.

I'm walking now, among the spring mosquitoes, those big #10s, along the moose trail, a shortcut to the hundred-yard-long run that marks South Fork's heart. Ten minutes away, I can hear the stream already, hissing, drumming, raising hell. My pulse pounds to match the current, despite my concerns that the water may run too high.

I am envisioning South Fork the way I first found it, with Trevor, as it will be three weeks from now: green, humid, shaded from direct sunlight by ferns, sinewy gray alder, grass tall enough to hide a brown bear. Years of fishing here have taught me that the lower run is best forded and fished from the north bank where broad gravel bars allow space for backcasts. Also, fish tend to hold against the shadier south bank and are more easily reached with crosscurrent casts.

Finally, the mosquitoes and the grasses along the moose trail part and South Fork appears. The water is high and swift, as I knew it would be, but it is translucent, meaning fish should be able to spot flies. I will be stuck fishing from the south bank, since my usual crossing now is chin-deep; besides, the north bank gravel bars that I normally cast from are flooded. The challenge will be in casting among dense alders. Meanwhile, clouds have gathered and it's starting to rain.

Within two summers, I came to realize that my hundred-yard slice of trout heaven was only one piece of a continuum that is much larger. In its entirety, South Fork is a conveyor, a pulsing measure of time and space, and in the way that a stream can never remain static, I myself sometimes grow restless. So one morning in the third summer, with a friend and a plan, I headed upstream, driven by a yen to see more.

Many anglers are explorers at heart, studying maps and remote streams, searching for something better. In a haphazard way, that's how Trevor and I discovered that first run on lower South Fork, where heavy rainbow trout sometimes break stout tippets, and wild roses and bluebells bloom pink and powder-blue, leaving the air fragrant with traces of cinnamon and natural sweetness that are a blend of earth, dew, and light.

To gain South Fork's more secluded reaches, Paul Cyr and I drove several miles upstream beyond a point where the stream and the road diverge. There, preparing to "bust brush" under skies that threatened at any time to split and gush water, I removed delicate camera equipment from my daypack and replaced it with rubber rain gear.

The descent into South Fork's wide, ancient bed came in varying increments, gradual in places, abrupt in others. It was stifling work in neoprene waders on a day that seemed to grow increasingly muggy and damp. Sweat in salty rivulets washed down our faces, bug dope burned our eyes. Mosquitoes howled.

Eventually we skidded down a final, shrubby, hundred-foot bluff to the valley floor, made our way through a cottonwood forest, and broke into a rock-walled gorge. There South Fork was wilder, bouncing and roaring over stony steps, resting in bottomless, trembling pools. A strip of wet sand revealed only the clawed tracks of a pigeon-toed grizzly.

King salmon, a dozen florid shadows long and thick as men's legs, held in a stretch of riffles. The water was so clear that depth perception was difficult; a rainbow, appearing black over glittering yellow sand, could have been a two-pounder holding shallow or a five-pounder hanging deep. Behind me, Paul said nothing. He was searching through polarized lenses for trout.

The first hole, a glassy slick tailing a midstream rock, was mine. My casts started out tentative as I probed the edges of the slick. Nothing. To avoid spooking fish, I next landed my streamer on top of the rock and with a twitch of my rod, slipped it gently into the slick's heart. The strike was violent. My leader was suddenly a taut piano wire burning upstream.

I don't know how many fish I've lost by turning away from the action to see if anyone else is looking. I realize that witnesses in these situations shouldn't matter, and chances are that anyone who does happen to get an eyeful will likely smirk while muttering curses. That's human nature. Yet, somehow, even the most cynical acknowledgments can slake certain insecurities. So, I turned my head. Paul was there, standing on the bank, watching. And sure enough, limp fly line hurled over my shoulder and my rod tip sprang back, the pressure of a broad-sided fish working the current abruptly gone. My mood darkened briefly, matched the brooding sky.

In a moment, Paul was downstream, at the head of a pool the size of a large living room. I made my way over bald cobbles as he stepped up on a boulder, stripped line from his reel and cast a big Egg-sucking Leech. The fly plopped into the pool's head, and I followed its progress, marked by green floating fly line. In that first drift, the line tightened suddenly and Paul hauled back. A silver flash flexed deep in the pool, a boil rolled on the surface. It was a big fish.

The battle, from my perspective as observer, was textbook, lacking only the dimension of sound lost to the drumming current. Paul's forearm bulged like a balloon about to pop as the fish, broad back cutting the surface in a ragged wake, surged downstream. Paul turned the fish at the tail of the pool, and it returned to the battle's starting point, then pivoted and ran again.

I'm not certain how much time passed before my friend knelt at the water's edge and lifted a heavy rainbow trout of seven or eight pounds from the pool. At that instant, the sun defied probability and poked through. Paul and the trout—the biggest of his life—glowed, the background a kaleidoscope of purple fireweed, green-leafed willows, stony canyon walls, and cottonwoods lit by the sun. It was a glorious photograph that, without my camera, went untaken.

At times like that it's difficult not to kick yourself, but "hero shots," "grip-and-grins," are of another dimension. The satisfaction is in knowing that a couple of guys can follow their hearts, weather be damned, and hook big fish in water that time, for the moment, has reserved.

Paul beamed, hovering over the pool, unaware of me or the sun. He lowered his hands into the water and the fish was gone.

Back on the lower run on this early summer day, I've waded up to my brisket across a swirling channel and am casting from a bar that is submerged in fast, knee-deep current. The rain has picked up, grown into a complete downpour, soaking my vest and sounding like heavy static. I fear the water might rise suddenly and trap me out here. So I reel in and wade against the powerful flow to the channel I crossed earlier.

The situation here is ticklish, one missed step and South Fork, my idyllic-trout-stream-gone-mad, will sweep me away, into a mass of trout-hiding, body-snagging logjams below. Drowning would be inevitable. Why, I wonder, do I put myself into such predicaments?

Waist-deep, a fly-rod's length from the alder jungle onshore, I hear something like a peal of distant thunder over the pounding rain. Death by lightning would at least be swifter, perhaps less terrifying, than going belly-up in frothing ice water. I pause, and it comes again, through the hissing rain, a resonating bass rumble that engulfs me as if I were standing in a cave. The sound is familiar.

While working at that lodge on the Brooks River years ago, I'd watched two brown bears fight over a salmon fishing hole. Boxing desperately on the riverbank a quarter mile away, they'd roared like lions. I was startled by the volume. Even from that distance, the ground had trembled: it was Brooks River brown bears in stereo.

Now, standing waist-deep in South Fork, swallowed in a cloudburst, I'm shocked to realize that the thunder is coming not from the sky, but from the alders before me. The rangers who patrolled Brooks River encouraged us to talk to bears, to identify ourselves as humans and avoid surprising the animals. So I'm backing toward midstream, to the riffle, hollering some sort of nonsense. The bear roars again and, for an instant, my heart stops.

I've brought no guns, not even a can of bear mace. I know better, but this was supposed to be a simple, after-work affair. Alaska is cruel to the careless. So now I'm trapped on the riffle in the downpour with time running out; a flash flood seems imminent. Swimming South Fork in its present ugly state is out of the question. My only way out, before the water gets any deeper, is across the channel where the roaring brown bear waits.

Minutes pass. I'm soaked, shivering, standing back at the channel's edge, shouting. The bear does not answer and I figure it's now or never. Struggling against the current, I reach the bank. Shouting some more and ducking among dripping alders, I'm soon on the moose trail, a trembling mass of goose flesh walking fast for the truck.

Adrenaline is the spice of life: you feel it when you lock eyes on the love of your life, when you hook a huge fish, or when your choices lie between drowning in your favorite trout stream or facing an eight-hundred-pound brown bear. Sometimes, when the wild forces here snatch you up, then let you go, an evening of fishing transcends the strike of fighting rainbow trout or rising grayling. At times likes this, in a place where a fish story can so swiftly turn into a bear tale, it is enough simply to be alive.

Summer Nights

There have been times when I've considered leaving Alaska, to escape for a few months or, perhaps, forever. But never in July. Notions of desertion are most nourishing in the dark days of December or during the long, heart-wrenching span of March. July is one of the main reasons many of us stay—along with May, June, August, and September.

The sun gets hot this time of year and the air smells of bug dope—pungent, tart. We have all-night barbecues and take long, early-morning walks on sleepy gravel roads. And, whenever possible, we step out to fish.

Last July, there was a period when the lower Susitna Valley steamed in a stretch of eighty-degree days. For lifelong Alaskans, it was too hot to sleep. We just lay in our beds, perspiring, while at 3 A.M. robins called in the birch trees outside our open windows.

I become sort of a night creature this time of year. The air seems fresher as it cools after 10 P.M. and my hay fever doesn't bother me as much. The world quiets and slows down, midnight birdcalls notwithstanding. And, best of all, the fishing gets better.

One evening, figuring a little missed sleep on a cool lake seemed better than a restless night in a sweaty bed, I took my float tube and fly rod and slid down the steep bluff overlooking a deep, kidney-shaped trout lake close to home. Pushed by an itchy mix of boredom and anticipation, I arrived too early— 9 P.M.—for decent fishing. The sun held brilliantly over the water, beaming from a cloudless sky. The lake was tepid as stale bath water; I'm guessing the surface temperature was around sixty-eight degrees.

A state fisheries biologist once told me that dissolved oxygen—the stuff fish filter from water through their gills—becomes scarce when water temperatures grow that warm. Fish, too, get scarce at such times, seeking oxygen in deeper, cooler, more mysterious parts of the lake; like aquatic vampires, they prowl the shallows only late at night.

I fished a weighted damselfly nymph for an hour with almost no luck, managing only to nab two or three six-inch parrs, and was preparing myself for the struggle back up the bluff when the last bit of sun melted into the trees. Almost instantly, the air grew much cooler than the water, creating pillows of mist that hung above the sleepy lake shore.

An aura of anticipation spiked the night, felt like that moment in a movie theater when the lights dim suddenly and the audience hushes. Things along the shoreline began to stir. Fish slurped and slapped the surface here and there, hesitantly at first, like the initial spitting drops of an evening cloudburst. Wood frogs grunted, muskrats paddled, and more fish jumped in an incredible crescendo of rhythm and life.

Summer nights, in their profound stillness, have a way of amplifying sound, and soon I could hear trout splashing and rolling clear across the lake. Large rainbows paced beneath alders and floating logs—places that earlier in the day offered shelter from the sun, where hapless bugs might fall upon the water. I decided to stay for the show.

The water was so still that stalking trout from my float tube became a challenge. The slightest ripple could put them down and I found it best to wait quietly twenty or thirty feet offshore and watch for fish to jump nearby. When a fish jumped twice in the same general location, I would move slowly into casting range and try to fool it. Often, those trout rose in the most God-awful places: next to snags under leafy plumes of alder or among innocent barricades of butter-blossomed lake lilies.

I hooked a couple twelve- to fourteen-inch rainbows on a yellow-bodied, brown-hackled dry fly of my own invention, but the fishing remained slow. Again, I was ready to wrap it up for the night when I saw a good trout of maybe two-and-a-half pounds jump close by, clearing the surface by at least a foot.

Slowly, taking care not to create any more ripples than necessary, I edged into casting range. As I closed in, the trout continued feeding, twice more leaping high out of the water. This allowed me to pinpoint the trout's lair: a pocket of dark water on the far side of a floating log, backed by overhanging brush. From a flyfisher's standpoint, it was a tricky, if not impossible, situation.

To reach the fish, I would have to put my fly down on the far side of the log. That meant my leader would actually lay across the log, a ridiculous position that still makes me wince. To land the fish, my only hope would be to strong-arm it around the log and paddle backward furiously, taking the battle out to the open lake. I knew that my chances of pulling off the plan were slim, but it was late and I had nothing more than a fly to lose.

Landing a fish, for an angler, is probably something like finishing a painting for an artist. (In the sense, as some artists say, that the moment you finish a painting, it ceases to be yours.) Your rod and your fly may serve as brushes, but the art is in your strategy. And ultimately, when a fish is gone—broken off, released, or gutted and fried—there's nothing left but a picture in your mind.

I accomplished the first phase of my plan on the third try, dropping my fly delicately onto the patch of black water. From there things happened fast. The trout took, grabbing my fly and breaching. Then it plunged straight down, and before I could muscle it into the main lake, it came up on my side of the log, splashed down on the far side and was suddenly gone, my broken leader still wrapped up among the gray splinters.

I've lost bigger fish, but never on a better night. I came away realizing that there is art, and often justice, in losing and enduring and knowing that nothing—not fish, paintings, nor winter—lasts forever. That's what makes Alaska's winters tolerable and July nights on Alaskan lakes particularly sweet.

Russian River Stones

L ooking back, I can see Uncle Sam, wide-eyed with panic,
drowning in a psychedelic funk. It is the age of tie-dye and
Vietnam; Watergate monopolizes the media in Anchorage and, I
learn later, around the world. For a little boy with crew-cut hair,
it's an unnerving period of social upheaval. I struggle to keep it
all in perspective.

The summer sun is warm, and my uncle, his two boys, and I
are climbing out of a red Volkswagen Bug, preparing to hike several miles into the upper Russian River. The trail always seems
long, but somewhere in the final mile, we can hear the river and
three listless, tired boys suddenly sprint the rest of the way in.

Over the rush of water, Uncle's faraway voice is indignant.
"You boys wait up; you're going to run into a bear! No fishing
until I get there."

For the moment, properly molding cured salmon roe onto #6
snelled hooks seems more important than Saigon or hippies
dancing naked in city parks.

The Russian is the fishing highlight of summer for us. Rainbow
trout longer than your arm hover in slicks behind midstream
rocks. Dolly Varden, fat and solid, shadow spawning red salmon.
I'm standing on a flat rock the size of a table top, casting a short
spinning rod outfitted with a chrome-plated, push-button Zebco
reel. My fingers and pants are smeared with salty orange roe; a
canvas creel hangs from one shoulder, bulging with small Dollys
and trout.

Water hisses around me, dashing among boulders, folding under logs. The air is fragrant with fish slime—an odor reminiscent of dew on crushed wild grass. There is no place I would rather be. Yet should someone ask me why I am fishing, I would likely appear puzzled before answering, *Because I like to.* In truth, I don't know why and probably would see little point in trying to find out. I have always fished; something about it makes me feel good.

Time occasionally scares the hell out of me, the way it flows so certainly, unstoppable, like a river. I caught myself the other day poking around in the right side of my head where a child narrator recalled a pleasant moment. Suddenly, the voice of a cynical man from the left side interrupted, shouting, *That happened twenty-five years ago!*

A quarter century? Couldn't be. So who is this little kid with the flute-like voice I sometimes hear in the current of a stream?

The Black Panthers have long since turned gray and the flower children's faces are wilting. Volkswagen no longer builds the old Bugs, but the Russian River remains a fishing highlight of summer. There are a few more anglers these days. Their hip-booted soles are wearing down the banks, and habitat loss is a growing concern. Still, there are plenty of trout, char, and salmon. The water remains clear as polished glass, revealing speckle-backed rainbows in midstream pools.

It's late June, and I'm sitting on a cottonwood log along the lower river, picking through a fly box, looking for the pattern I will use to start the day. Fishing here was simpler when my selections were limited to single eggs or roe.

Impulsively, I pluck from the box an orange-bodied streamer with a white marabou tail. There's nothing sexy about a Battle

Creek Special, a bright, hairy cross between a Woolly Bugger and a gob of salmon roe, but I know it's a lethal pattern in September when salmon eggs and bits of flesh from spawned-out salmon drift downstream.

Even in June the Battle Creek Special is a solid choice, as scores of freshly filleted red salmon carcasses—tossed into the river by meat-fishing crowds—whirl by in the current, stacking against snags and washing up on gravel bars. But it reminds me very much of bait, as I suppose it should, and my desire today is to draw fish to the surface. There is no snobbishness in this wish, just a self-imposed challenge, more perhaps for variety's sake than anything else.

So now I'm looking for a message from the sky, and I don't have to search long. Backlit by the caramelized light of late afternoon, legions of tiny bugs flail and flap in helter-skelter flight. They light anxiously on my fly rod, my vest, my face. Resisting the urge to swat, I pull a bug off my cheek. Lime-green, the size of a mosquito, proportionately long and thin like a twig, it is a Russian River stonefly.

Russian River stones hatch regularly throughout the summer and into fall. One day in September, armed with an eight-weight rod and large, weighted streamers, I stood for half an hour watching an eddy where a trout slurped hapless green stoneflies. There in the height of salmon egg season, I drifted a Glo-bug by the fish, but it showed no interest. Even though I caught plenty of fish that day, several fine rainbows and Dollys and a deep-bodied silver salmon that grabbed a Marabou Muddler, I still regretted not having a floating line, light leader, and #14 stonefly with elk-hair wings and dubbed, neon-green body.

That's why today I'm prepared. The Battle Creek goes back where I found it, to wait for a day when few bugs are hatching, and I choose instead one of my hand-tied stonefly imitations.

Weaved lovingly the previous March, my Russian River Stone is something less than an exact imitation, but it is my baby and I knot it faithfully onto my leader.

Stoneflies, mixed now with a good hatch of caddis, continue to flutter over the stream. Sunshine dapples the jungle of grasses, mountain ash, cow parsnip, birch, and spruce trees that frame the banks in vivid greens. The place smells fresh but familiar, and the rushing current reminds me that I am *alive* and that still there is no place I would rather be at this moment than right here, right now, fishing.

I've often suspected that life is a river that runs in a circle; no matter where you start, you seem to end up in the same place. Nearly thirty years after Apollo 11, here I am, somewhere between the baby boomers and Generation X, still fishing at the place where, for me, time began. And if time has shifted my means, the end remains the same. I fish to gain admission to a timeless world. I fish because I like to.

June nights on the Russian River are acoustic compositions of hissing water and varied thrushes that lurk unseen, piercing the current's carbonated s-s-s-s with eerie, buzzing trills. The air, dense and cool, seems turbid at midnight; the atmosphere, in night's tradition, is mysterious, vaguely surreal. Upstream from the Russian's confluence with the Kenai River, the river is a sky-mirroring channel of dim light framed by silhouetted trees. On windless, rainless nights, darting shapes that are silent and that are not birds, flutter in spasmodic flight across this channel. Like the trout, they feed on summer's spate of bugs—stoneflies, caddis, mosquitoes, moths.

One evening I followed my friend Tony Route as he waded along the lower Russian River, working the dregs of a caddis hatch. Marty Sherman, fifty-ish, an Alaska-born editor of a fly-fishing magazine, also was along, and we watched quietly as our friend cast a thick rod rigged with a waking dry fly the size of a hummingbird. The fly was most likely a Bomber, but in the murky light I couldn't be sure.

When I wondered aloud why he used such large flies and heavy tackle, Tony, his face lit faintly by the embers of his pipe, glanced up as if to see whether I was serious.

I was.

Tony's face fell, became grave, and then he turned away, pointed toward a pool downstream.

"Thirty-inch rainbows lay in that hole," he said. Tony looked back at me over his shoulder, perhaps to see if I was laughing. I was not. The conviction in his voice, the way his pipe burned brighter as he stared over the water, left no doubt that he *believed.*

He went on, "A couple years ago, about this time of night, I felt a 'tick' when I was casting—like I'd clipped my rod on a branch. Then, something dropped out of the sky, landed in the water by my feet." He paused, smoke rising through the dusk, gathering above his head like a phosphorescent halo. "I'd cold-cocked a little brown bat."

Marty, silent up to that point, spoke suddenly, "Joyce once *hooked* a bat in midair." He was referring to his wife, also a hard-bitten flyfisher. "The thing took a dry fly at the end of her back-cast. Had a heck of a time getting it loose."

Tony sucked on his pipe and nodded. The sky suddenly seemed darker, the river louder.

"The current caught the bat," he continued, pointing again downstream, "swept it over that hole. There was a splash …"

He raised his eyebrows and eyeballed me suspiciously.

"And the bat," he said solemnly, "was gone."

Thirty-inch trout in the Russian River are intriguing, but not incredibly surprising. The river has a long history of monster rainbows; a thirty-three-inch hog, for example, hung in the 1930s on the wall of Seward's Van Gilder Hotel. Many others likely ended up as steaks, fried over birchwood fires in an era pre-dating catch-and-release.

Once, on a drizzling September morning a couple years ago, I was spooled by a large rainbow where the Russian meets the Kenai. I was drifting a Battle Creek Special through knee-deep riffles below a mass of spawning red salmon. The strike was stunning, like a thunderbolt, and I knew immediately that my five-weight rod was too light for the welling fight. I held on and attempted for a moment to stay my ground, figuring I'd hooked a fresh silver salmon.

Then the fish, a rainbow trout nearly three feet long, leapt into the air in midstream and skipped on its tail across the riffles. My twelve-pound backing was too light for the combined power of that trout and the relentless thrust of the Kenai River, so when the fish inevitably turned and ran straight downstream, I pointed my rod tip and gripped the final inches of my fly line.

⟞⟝

There is more to the lower Russian River than bats at midnight and monster rainbow trout. Embedded in the soil—a composite of glacial silt, volcanic ash, and desiccated salmon a thousand years old—rest the bones and blood of people who fished the Russian sixty centuries before Christ was born. Sometimes when you're alone, usually between crowd-drawing blasts of fresh-run sockeyes, the river's lower quarter mile seems to pulse with a supernatural energy that is almost palpable, a dance of spirits, played to the cadence of the hustling river and your own pounding heart.

In the morning, when the living earth grows still, salmon with their brains and bellies ripped out lie scattered among the cobbles of the lower Russian. Clawed paw prints twice as wide and half again as long as an average man's boot print, the work of bears prowling. Some native Alaskans believed that the hides of brown bears covered the spirits of men. The connection between the salmon, the paw prints, and the ruins of a lost culture is irresistible.

On a spruce-studded terrace overlooking the junction of the Russian and Kenai rivers, clusters of shallow depressions are visible beneath grasses and yellow wild poppies. These are the remnants of the Kenaitze Dena'ina Indians who, as proven by chalky bones and stone blades plucked from the loam, first settled along the Russian 8,000 years ago. Salmon were the Indians' main food source and the hundreds of small depressions in the earth today mark cache pits where fish were stored for winter use. Larger, rectangular pits represent homesites where families wintered.

Life for the Kenaitze Dena'ina probably remained simple along the lower Russian River until something over 200 years ago. That's when the first tourists began arriving on the Kenai Peninsula, including Captain James Cook, who in 1778 explored with his sailing ships, *Discovery* and *Resolution*, the waters surrounding the mouth of the Kenai River. But Cook never actually saw the nameless salmon stream we would one day call the Russian. He was mostly interested in the glory of a northwest passage discovery. Seventy years later a group of prospectors from Russia found the river and sluiced its gravel bottom. The Russians departed two years later with eighty-four ounces of gold. The stream, by attrition, was named for them.

In 1867, Russia, having long laid claim to Alaska, sold the territory to the United States for two cents an acre. The Kenaitze Dena'ina, of course, had nothing to say of the transaction, but they were eventually recognized and included in the 1880 U.S.

census. By that time the Kenaitze Dena'ina of the Russian River, ravaged like their Lower Forty-eight counterparts by epidemics of influenza, smallpox, and measles, numbered a mere forty-four souls.

Those final Russian River Kenaitze, sick and dying, pulled stakes in 1884 and migrated, in desperation, fifty miles to the mouth of the Kenai River. An obvious void must have been visible to Joe Cooper, prospector and founder of today's sportfishing and resort community of Cooper Landing, when he entered the region that same year to plant his own sluice boxes in the bed of the Russian River.

The river today remains an anglers' paradise partly because it never gave up enough gold to encourage large-scale mining. After Cooper, however, a few miners and big-game guides stayed on. By 1938, a road was built connecting Cooper Landing to the seaport of Seward, then the main access point from Outside to southcentral Alaska. Tales of incredible fishing for rainbow trout, Dolly Varden, and salmon on the Russian River began to leak out and made their way into the pages of outdoor magazines. Ten years later the road was extended to Kenai, and in 1951 the highway to Anchorage was opened.

Now the lower Russian is Alaska's most popular, most crowded sport fishery. Trampled banks are fenced off to protect natural forbs and shrubs that anchor soils and provide cover for rainbow trout and young salmon. More than a hundred years following the migration of the last Dena'ina, the place continues to lose its innocence. Perhaps, in the karmic way that time and actions evolve and come full-circle, a heart-breaking form of natural justice is unfolding. Much has changed; mirthful spirits laugh.

Still, it is good to know that thirty-inch, bat-eating monsters remain.

At 3 P.M., the sun blazes high and surprisingly hot over the Russian River's Pink Salmon parking lot. Marty, Tony, and I are gathered around a minivan, pulling on waders, slipping fly rods from aluminum tubes.

The night before we had floated the upper Kenai, starting at 7 P.M., among flurries of hatching caddis and stoneflies that fluttered over the river in the eye of a surly evening squall. We put in across from the Kenai–Russian River confluence and bobbed downstream, stopping at select gravel bars and eddies to fish, mostly for fresh red salmon. We caught many salmon using various streamers, although Marty found #8 chartreuse Hare's Ear Nymphs to be particularly hot medicine. At one point during the caddis hatch, I pulled out a light rod and hooked a small rainbow on an Elk Hair Caddis. We did not turn in until after 2 A.M.

Today it feels good to leave the hot blacktop and enter the shady forest. Along the river, the air is cool and wet. Within an hour, my friends and I have split up to fish, hiking upriver to remote pools and falls.

This is the Russian River of old, a quaint, shady, wild stream of ferns and veiled sunlight. But a mile or two below, the arrival of two summer red-salmon runs marks an annual eight-week-long free-for-all—a circus of bumping elbows, tangled lines, and snagged cheeks. It is an ugly scene, crowded, a scarring contradiction.

Thankfully, the spell is cast only so far along the river as salmon concentrate and people care to walk. A few of both appear scattered upstream, but not enough to spoil the mood. I'm standing knee-deep in a sunlit riffle overlooking a shaded pool formed by boulders and flotsam. A brown caddisfly waddles across my hand as I tie on a #8 Muddler. Tony, who is something of a Russian River trout expert, tells me that fish here key best to out-sized dry flies. On a floating line with a nine-foot leader, I

figure the weightless Muddler might imitate a magnum caddisfly
in a hatch that is gaining intensity as the afternoon wanes.

I may be a little undergunned, casting a four-weight graphite
in waters where bat-eating monsters lurk. But I have landed silver salmon and even a few steelhead on this little rod. Here in the
Russian's swift, plunging current, I will keep the fish pointed upstream, let the river wear them out.

My Muddler bobs nicely at the head of the pool. I'm holding
my rod in the air, high, like a torch, to keep the fast water on my
side of the pool from stealing my line. The fly drifts the length of
the pool, perhaps twelve feet, before it is sucked through the tailout and into a foaming pocket at the base of a chute. I'm gathering line for another cast when I feel a yank. Suddenly, my line is
cutting downstream through choppy rapids, and the realization
dawns on me that if I care to see what has taken my fly, I had better shake a leg downstream.

The struggle is short and sweet, complicated only by the dashing current and some damming logs. The fish, a trout, thirteen or
fourteen inches long, feels as good in my hand today as it would
have decades ago. But today I have no creel; I'm happy watching
the trout revive itself in the shallows, gills pumping, tail wagging.
As I watch, the trout's eyes seem to grow abruptly wider, the
body grows rigid, as if something inside has suddenly fallen into
place. In a wink, the fish is gone, off into the deep shadows.

I'm stepping out of the water when Tony, clad in khaki from
billed cap to socks, appears without warning among waist-high
ferns. We smile and talk about the fishing—no hogs today, but it is
early. Somewhere within our developing bond lurks a thread of
apprehension, a slight, unspoken rivalry. Upstream, below a rocky
gorge where ouzels nest, we sit on a boulder munching candy bars
and sipping soda pop. Tony mentions in vague terms a wonderful
stream in remote southwest Alaska. He visits the stream each fall

for a week, he says, adding in more specific terms the size and number of large rainbow trout he catches and the fine ptarmigan hunting there.

I'm no better, ever anxious to share tales of Susitna Valley streams I have discovered. I had fished the Valley earlier in the week, caught some truly fine trout.

"Really?" Tony asks, taking the bait. "I haven't spent much time there. How big?"

"What?"

"How big are the trout you catch there in the Valley?"

"Nothing over ten pounds," I answer. "My friend Paul caught one Wednesday that would've gone eight."

We continue our lunch in silence. It is a sort of checkmate.

We're gathered at the first pool on the lower river at 10 P.M., more hungry than tired. It goes without saying that we will stop at Gwinn's Lodge on our way back to our camp at Quartz Creek. Gwinn's, a weathered log throwback to Cooper Landing's early days, is where hungry anglers gather for cheeseburgers and cold beer. If you fish the Russian or Upper Kenai River much at all, you will likely run into an old friend or two sitting under the massive stuffed rainbow trout mounted on a polished spruce purlin.

The burgers will fill gnawing voids, as will the first sweating pitcher of beer. Talk will probably turn to future plans—a float trip down the Goodnews River, scheduled for August when the silvers are running; a grouse hunt with so-and-so and his Springer bitch on opening day six weeks away. When the second pitcher is poured, cold, wet, and fizzy, conversation will loosen up. Maybe I'll offer to take my friends along to one of my Susitna Valley streams. Perhaps Tony will invite me along to that tundra river where bucket-mouthed trout munch swimming lemmings and ptarmigan hunting in the willows is fantastic on sunny afternoons.

You never know. A couple of beers following a day of fishing have a way of tearing down little walls. Anyhow, the company is guaranteed to be good, the conversation interesting, and new schemes will hatch, like Russian River stones.

Dinosaur Fish

I am harnessed in my float tube in the shallows of a Susitna Valley lake, fighting a queer panic as weeds grope my frantic legs. I am haunted by photographs, tacked up in local fly shops and air taxi offices, of dinosaur fish, living fossils pulled from this lake and others nearby.

Long and heavy, the biggest were dragged in writhing and glowering on stout, steel-leadered lines rigged with halibut hooks and bait herring. I can't help wondering if the shiny buckles on my swim fins might seem tempting to creatures with mouths wide enough to swallow basketballs.

Flyfishing for northern pike in the Susitna Valley, though catching on, is still considered offbeat. I don't know anyone dedicated purely to pike, although it's fun to imagine a few such oddballs exist. This is the perfect sport for deep-rooted nonconformists who shun name-brand gear and neon-colored vests— hard-living, Captain Ahab types in patched waders, searching for the fifty-pounder that everyone believes lurks in lakes like Donkey, Flathorn, and Whiskey.

If nothing else, casting streamers dressed on gaping #3/0 hooks and tied to braided metal leaders lends a perverse diversity to flyfishing Valley lakes. Sure, four-pound rainbow trout are a kick, but with pike we're talking about fish that bite back and may go ten times that size. This is stillwater flyfishing with a wicked edge.

Rafts of bluebills huddle offshore, bobbing in light chop, resigned to a stubborn downpour. They're probably safe out there in deep water; still, I wouldn't want to be a duck here. A friend pass-shooting on a Minto Flats pike slough near Fairbanks once told of dropping a green-winged teal over open water. Before he could reload and wade out to retrieve his duck, he heard a furious splash and looked up to find the bird gone.

My lake is a lead-gray mirror shattered by the rain. Water rolls off my visor, thumps on the rubber hood over my neck. Rain matters little to me today, since float-tubing requires that you be half underwater to begin with. I'm more concerned about what might be down there, in the black water, eyeballing my dangling legs.

Forty-five years ago, a bucket biologist, quite probably casting a red-and-white spoon into a tamarack-fringed bog on the north side of the Alaska Range, caught a tub full of green, snaky fish with crude duck-billed heads and mouths bristling with raking teeth. Hours later, that tub of swirling, snapping swamp sharks found its way to the south side of the range and into the pristine waters of Bulchitna Lake. For the first time in history, northern pike were Susitna Valley residents.

Progeny of that introduction spilled into the Susitna River drainage when Bulchitna overflowed in a subsequent spring runoff. Northerns—including individuals spanning four feet and topping thirty pounds—continue to spread throughout the Susitna Valley, thriving on diets rich in native rainbow trout, grayling, and five species of young salmon. The state record stands at thirty-eight pounds, but Alaska's best pike water remains remote and unfished; surely larger—perhaps *much* larger—fish exist.

Black spruce along the shoreline appear and vanish as the muskeg smolders in brooding mist. Outwardly, Susitna Valley lakes invaded by pike show little change. A lily garden lit by an errant shaft of sunlight suggests tranquillity, an impressionistic,

Monet-esque illusion. Once upon a time, a Marabou Lake Leech cast here might have fooled a fat, cruising rainbow trout. But life has dealt the rainbows and us lemons.

So I'm here to make the best of a world that is always changing, searching for a new twist with a tart streamer fashioned the night before from saddle hackles dyed yellow and red. Needle-nosed pliers, heavy steel jobs, are used to attach flies to my thirty-pound-test "Iron Thread" leader. My rod is the same one I use for silver salmon in August, a four-piece eight-weight, nine feet long, with enough backbone to cast big hooks and take on all but the biggest, nastiest fish in the lake. I figure if it's too big to catch with this outfit, I'd rather not drag it up to my tube in the first place.

The Susitna Valley is a soggy place, a massive composite of muskegs, lakes, creeks, and rivers, all loosely connected. During spring breakup, these connections dilate in the wake of a receding snowpack. Moose trails between ponds become temporary canals; muskegs swell, saturated like paddies, knee-deep, weeping into streams. In a dry summer, many of these links will fade and disappear altogether. But by then, it is too late.

That ol' Bulchitna Lake pike stocker probably had no idea how devastating his illegal introduction might someday be. In late April or early May, when winter's ice turns rubbery and melts in the glare of a warming sun, northern pike gather in weedy shallows to spawn. They are prolific creatures; a gravid, twenty-five-pound hen (northern pike females live longer and grow larger than males) may drop a half-million eggs that settle and cling to sedges, rocks, and water-logged sticks. Within a month, young pike hatch, instant carnivores preying on dragonfly nymphs, caddis larvae, and scuds. As they grow, potential prey grows also and includes fish (particularly whitefish, gray-ling, trout, young salmon, and other pike), voles, shrews, shore-birds, small ducks, muskrats … any living thing they can catch and swallow.

Dave Rutz, a state sportfish biologist in Palmer, spent years studying Susitna Valley northern pike, netting and tagging them, analyzing stomach contents, mapping their malignant move-ments through those saturated lowlands. He recorded the de-struction, charted forty or fifty Valley lakes where rainbow trout have been wiped out completely. Most frightening is the devas-tating potential pike have on local salmon stocks. Rutz describes surveys at Hewitt Lake where scores of pike congregate at the lake outlet to gobble young salmon on their way to sea.

"I had one pike that was maybe twenty-two inches," Rutz says. "He had twenty sockeye smolt inside of him."

But sockeye salmon are the least of Rutz's worries. Sockeyes, known regionally as reds, often rear in big, deep lakes (rare in the Valley) where they can escape northern pike by feeding in deep water. Rutz's concern, the kind of dread that prods hard-working biologists awake in the night, is the bite pike are taking out of sil-ver salmon runs. The Susitna Valley's shallow ponds, lakes, and weedy sloughs provide perfect rearing habitat for young silver salmon—and classic hunting grounds for hungry pike.

"It's a total overlap," says Rutz. "And the pike are winning out in all those shallow lakes and slow-water sloughs and slow-water creek systems."

Pike, salmon, and trout seem to co-exist tolerably enough in parts of southwest Alaska where large, deep lakes and swift streams keep pike at bay. Still, as Rutz says, you have to wonder if coho fishing would be a little better if pike weren't in those systems.

Some people apparently prefer northern pike to rainbow trout and arctic grayling. Contemporaries of the Bulchitna bucket biologist continue to dump pike in landlocked lakes throughout southcentral Alaska. When in 1994 rumors of pike catches in landlocked Knik Lake west of Wasilla reached state biologist Al Havens, now retired, he quietly stepped out one evening and set a few fish traps. Next day, Havens was stunned to find five northern pike in his traps. One of them went thirty-two inches.

Pike also have been reported recently in Sand Lake in Anchorage, Fire Lake near Chugiak, and in several landlocked Susitna Valley lakes. These lakes could be cleaned out simply enough with poison, restocked with trout, grayling, landlocked salmon. But there's nothing to stop subsequent illegal introductions of pike.

As for the Susitna River drainage, pike now are far too widespread for Rotenone or anything else. They've impregnated the natural fabric, become part of the local scheme. Commercial fishermen working off the Susitna River's mouth have pulled pike from gill nets set for salmon. Dave Rutz says these fish are tough, able to tolerate brackish water. Trout and salmon lovers fear the pike infection will spread throughout Cook Inlet. Already, word has them in the Little Susitna River drainage, Big Lake, and Meadow Creek. In the end, there can be no more surprises. Northerns have survived time, anglers, and ice ages. Pike are powerful medicine. They are here to stay.

The first strike comes within a half-dozen casts. POW! The fish hits like a hammer or a missile exploding on impact. The struggle is frenzied, a bull-dogging, head-shaking tug of war that begins with a splash near the surface and then works down, toward the deep stuff, making my drag shriek, my rod jolt. Even so, I know this is not one of the big ones and, secretly, I'm relieved. I'm accustomed to tubing for trout and grayling—better to work my way up gradually.

Inside of a minute, maybe half that long, the fight fizzles. My line falls slack even reeling as fast as I can, and the fish submits, glides straight for my tube. A couple feet from my paddling fins, the fish seems suddenly to recognize the gravity of the moment and again the fight is on. This sequence is repeated two or three times before I can grab the fly with my pliers and lift the pike clear of the water.

Three-and-a-half, maybe four pounds, twenty-six- to twenty-eight-inches long, with cold, glaring eyes and bony teeth extending like tusks from the lower jaw: I'm looking at a killer.

Trout and grayling, hooked and brought to hand, are frightened creatures—you can see the fear in their rolling eyes. But pike offer nothing. The eyes are emotionless, robotic. Yet, if you can find your way beyond the stare and the toothy, underslung steel-trap jaws through which ducklings, muskrats, and all resident species of fish perish, northern pike own a certain, hand-painted beauty with their tough leather skin smooth as a wallet, their olive or emerald green flanks dappled with bars and spots the color of sunlight winking on pond bottoms.

Built to lunge, northerns lack the stamina and tenacity of rainbow trout. Where trout and salmon are generally elliptical, pike are shaped more like dashes—streamlined, like aquatic cheetahs. From the bank, they sometimes pass for logs or sticks in the shallows, hovering motionless among the weeds until some wriggling life form passes by.

With a twist of my pliers, the pike falls back into the lake. I'd noticed a scar above its ventral fin, ragged, pink, a sign that it has escaped something bigger. The thought makes my dancing legs tingle.

It's got to be hell living at the bottom of the food chain. Every movement is measured, weighed against the possibility of imminent, violent death. Around here, red-backed voles comprise the chain's rock-bottom link. They skitter like wind-blown leaves through the tall grasses and along muskeg edges, short-tailed, hamster-like rodents, with black shining eyes and soft, red-brown fur. Damn near everything out here eats them: owls, magpies, weasels, martens, foxes, wolves, eight-hundred-pound grizzly bears. Fish. Big rainbows take voles as they swim like fuzzy corks on lakes and slow streams. And, of course, so do pike.

The biggest pike in the Valley often are taken on topwater flies. A local expert who mans the counter at Three Rivers Fly and Tackle in Wasilla recommends a fluffy muskrat-fur dressing big enough to swab a chimney.

I have watched pike attack a red-and-white bass popper. The popper puttered innocently along a deep, dark drop-off and was sucked up abruptly in a slashing, boiling strike. Too, I have seen pike leap out of the water like cobras to come down on poppers stripped idly among midlake lilies.

Voles, poppers, big-assed northern pike—it all came together a couple of winters back as I picked through the cardboard box where I keep saddle hackles, chenille, hanks of bear hair, and grouse skins. A patch of moose mane dyed a familiar burnt sienna caught my eye, along with a sample box of stingers, wicked, double-barbed hooks made of strong, light wire—perfect ingredients for spinning floating moose-hair voles.

I kept one of those voles in a fly box for two years before the

right time finally came. Dropped off for the day by an air taxi on
a nameless Susitna Valley lake, I spent the day with my father-in-
law, casting Muddlers in a nearby stream to mean-spirited rainbow trout. The day was hot and muggy, as they sometimes are in
the Valley in July. Our pilot had an old canoe stashed in the
brush near the lake. He encouraged us to paddle around for pike,
if the trout fishing was slow

"There're some dandies in there!" he said.

The trout fishing was not fantastic, a risk you take when you
choose at random an unnamed trout stream coursing the front
lines of a pike invasion. The fish we did catch, however, were
beefy, averaging sixteen inches or more, with some topping
twenty. I figured the lack of small trout had something to do with
certain residents of the lily-choked lake that bled into our creek.

Walt, who grew up among brookies, brown trout, and small
streams in eastern Ontario, fell in love with the gravel bars and
rainbows, scattered as they were, of that narrow Susitna Valley
stream. He was, however, no fan of canoes. So an hour before our
plane was to return, I left Walt casting happily in a sprightly,
alder-shaded run and hiked upstream to the lake.

For a while, I didn't even fish, just sat in the canoe and glided
over the windless lake, smooth and tannic. The water looked like
polished cherry wood. A cow moose chugged across the lake's
far side, only her head and hump showing, escaping the mosquitoes and horseflies that swarmed in the heat. Ducks were suspiciously few. At one point, paddling just offshore, I looked
through the glare into a sedge-lined drop-off and glimpsed a
moss-backed, cream-spotted torpedo as long and thick as my leg.
It was time.

I tied my vole, roughly-clipped, yet rodent-like in an impressionistic sort of way, to a leader of twelve-pound-test monofilament. (I'd been focused on trout and had forgotten my wire

leader.) I ripped line off the Lamson in yard-long pulls, holding my rod between my knees, paddling some to keep up the momentum. The pike I'd seen cruising the shoreline was long gone, but there would be others.

Soon my vole trailed the canoe on forty or fifty feet of line, a pathetic little creature that appeared from my vantage to be strikingly authentic. I hadn't paddled long when I heard a splash, like the slap of a beaver tail. I turned and saw the wake behind my fly. I dropped the paddle, picked up my rod, and watched the water explode. The Lamson screamed, the rod bucked, and for the moment, my hands were full.

A vicious energy rumbled through my eight-weight, made it tremble right down to the cork. The fish tore straight down, shaking its head. For a time, I thought I might get spooled, but I braked the reel with my palm, and the canoe gave some, like a buoy attached to a whale. Inside of five minutes, pumping and grinding, shirtless and sweating in the hot July sun, I turned the pike and led it to the canoe's side. I felt my eyes widen when I realized I was attached to a mean-looking fish three feet long and deep-bodied—ten pounds, easy.

For a while, I sat there wondering. Two thick pike fillets might grill up nicely; it wouldn't hurt the area's waning trout population. But I had no pliers to grip the double-barbed #3/0 hook and no net to scoop up the fish. I could see my vole, product of a winter night's work, beloved sum of my own creative spark, lodged deep inside that thorny mouth.

Reasoning that twelve-pound test should easily hold a ten-pound pike lifted out of the lake, I gripped my leader and pulled. Out came the pike's head, then the gills, the pectorals. I could feel the dead weight. Then the pike thrashed, one violent motion of raking teeth, and in a splash, it was gone. I leaned over the side and looked down into the brown, smoky water. For a moment the pike lay there, a grim shadow, sulking, the tail of my vole sticking out its jaw like a well-chewed maduro. Then the shadow faded, grew smaller, fainter, dissolving like a mirage into the cool darkness.

The lake today is too ravaged by rain and wind for surface action; the litter mates of my prototype vole remain huddled in a float tube pocket. I'm sticking with a Seaducer, a red-and-yellow salt-water streamer that on days like this is death on pike.

I'm into another fish inside of five minutes and another after that and then another, all three-pound hammer handles, clones born seemingly of the same womb. Each savagely punishes my streamers, which rarely survive three attacks. They malevolently lunge, fight, relent for a moment, and fight again. A couple, hooked firmly in those mangling jaws, actually leap, like perverse, snaky trout.

The fishing is so fast that, hours later, I am suddenly conscious of the rain that has fallen without pause all day long. In fact, everything in the world beyond casting and hooking and playing pike among swamp grass and Labrador Tea rushes back in a massive revelation. I guess you could say that, for now, I've chosen my reality, alone in a world away from my demons, whatever they may be, fighting other demons, more tangible, among the lilies and sedges.

For a moment, with a fly rod and patched waders, I am on the fringe, where fashion doesn't count and a guy casting big flies on metal leaders remains a sort of pioneer.

One Enchanted Evening

We met one January in a tropical place where the water is blue and bright as sapphire. I'd sipped a sweet rum drink and watched her attempt her first skeet shoot off the stern of a great, white cruise ship.

Ten clay birds soaring fast over the calm sea, ten one-ounce loads of #8 lead shot vanishing into the Caribbean sky. She never touched the first nine. But the last one was different. She shouldered the 20-gauge pump without apprehension, called out smiling, leaned into the shot, and popped the bird into dust. The crowd watching burst into a spontaneous cheer.

Six months later, she left her home in Canada to visit me in Alaska. We climbed mountains in the Chugach Range on hot June days and shared deep-fried halibut-on-a-stick on the wharf in Homer. Then, one cool, dusky night dip-netting salmon in a Copper River eddy, I made up my mind for good. Only Alaska residents may dip-net the Copper, but she was happy to sit alone on the cold gravel, watching, and she appeared at my side to help when I scooped up a king salmon buck so heavy that it bent my net handle. She stuck with me into the wee hours, through a red salmon here, another there, despite a miserable glacial wind blowing in from the peaks.

Finally, I had known that it was enough. We married seven months later.

It may not be the most romantic love story ever told, but the setting and the timing, the ultimate decision, were distinctly Alaskan. Call it destiny. I am, after all, a product of this place.

A lot of water has since flowed down the Copper. There have been some changes, the inevitable kind that come with marriage and children. But that core of light that comes from the heart and glows in the eyes remains.

Now it is July and North Fork, a freestone creek north of the house, is running along like an old friend, cheerful, singing quietly to itself over boulders and beds of gravel. The time is late evening and I'm standing with Sonnie, my wife, on a gravel bar in the mandarin light of the low-riding sun.

In the fashion of sunlit Alaska summer nights, the atmosphere is subdued, hushed. Even the sound of the current seems muted. Still, life this time of year never stops completely. Robins and thrushes huddled on the spruce tops call out infrequently, as if to announce, "Ten o'clock and all is well." Caddis are hatching upstream and down, fluttering over the black water, among bankside willows.

Sonnie's casting a five-weight into the heart of the hatch, smoothly as she can, concentrating less on the grayling rising in front of her than on her backcast and the wall of clinging brush lining the bar behind her. She is nervous, and that's unfortunate, because fishing tonight should be about tranquillity, in line with the moment and this gentle stream. But really, it's all my fault.

A friend who flyfishes once suggested that we would be wise to trade wives for a day when we show them the ropes of our sport.

"We're more patient with others," he'd said. And he's right. But tonight it's just Sonnie and me. My frustration over some minor points in her casting has left her self-conscious. So I've resolved to back off, letting her learn some of those things only experience can teach. Like on that dreamy Caribbean afternoon shooting skeet.

It's nice to have Sonnie along. I've been missing her lately, running off after work to do most of my fishing alone. One evening last week, after our toddler daughters were down for the night, Sonnie and I had sat out on the porch watching birch leaves rattle in a warm breeze, enjoying a stillness that has grown rare in the wake of child rearing. We sat for a long time without speaking, then Sonnie started recalling out loud this or that event that had occurred before the girls were born.

"I used to fish with you then ..." Her voice had trailed off.

When I was a boy, fishing and hunting seemed the exclusive domains of men. That perception, of course, was bound to change. When I was ten years old, my sister suddenly was allowed—no, *encouraged*—to come along on a week-long caribou hunt. This happened at about the same time Bobby Riggs and Billy Jean King were duking it out on the tennis court. The sexes were at war.

For a day or two, out there on the tundra in a windswept world of caribou herds and ice-cold rivers, I'd maintained an attitude that females were a contradiction to the outdoors scene. My sister shrugged me off, caught a few fish on dry flies, helped butcher caribou in the field, and enjoyed the time of her life. Gradually I accepted her being out there, gently appreciating her as much as an older brother can a pesky younger sister. And by the end of the week, my journey was pretty well over. Gender, I'd discovered, had no bearing on Royal Coachman flies or the nostalgic smells of willows and burnt gun powder.

Now grayling are rising in front of my wife. They are tolerant creatures, and greedy, too. I think that, for beginning Alaskan flyfishers, they are perhaps the best teachers of all.

Sonnie's cast slaps the water like the tail of a beaver. It makes me wince, but I don't say a word. Not that it would matter. She's tuned me out completely, focusing now on her drift and the feeding fish. I can see that everything's all wrong—the belly in her line causing her dry fly to drag across the current like a speed boat. I want to say something, but I've already said enough. Suddenly the water boils, then breaks. Sonnie doesn't know to set the hook, but she doesn't have to. The grayling runs with the fly and hooks itself.

The struggle is brief. My wife slips the hook from the grayling's mouth and watches the fish go. Then she looks up, beaming, and the silence of the night is broken for good.

Little Mysteries

Distant thunder. You can feel it in your chest, sense it beneath your feet, hear it rumbling far away. But this time it is very close.

It starts as I wade a tailout with my fly rod and step carelessly into the foot of a pool that is torpid and deep, like a great oval bath tub. The thunder builds, the pool trembles visibly, and then it erupts in wakes that slap the red sand banks.

Below the surface, the pool is alive; scores of panicked bodies swirl like leaves in a wind. Pink salmon. I've spooked them; hundreds of hard-nosed, hump-backed bodies slam helter-skelter into the pool's sides and bottom as they flee, creating a sound that resembles, in a muted sort of way, the ruckus of a great caribou herd startled by wolves.

Ten years ago Prince William Sound was no place for smoking, much less fishing. The water was flammable. Waterfowl were "gooey ducks." Enough North Slope crude oozed among the bays of hemlock and mussel-encrusted slate to keep a Subaru station wagon lubed for 26,000,000 highway miles (or 110 family vacations to the moon). The wilderness was toxic and smelled like a filthy refinery.

That spring the Sound had lost its innocence in the dying gasps of 5,000 sea otters and 350,000 birds. (*Save the animals, wear synthetic fur! And where, by the way, does fake fur come from?*) I saw the mess firsthand, got a bearcat of a headache breathing the petroleum fumes. No birds sang.

We have since learned that the Sound is healing, the scars fading like tears drying on the cheeks of a sulking child. But I've been away for a while, haunted by what I saw on Culross Island, Applegate, and Eshamy Bay. I remember too clearly the way it was before the poisoning.

Along this tannic brook forty miles east of Bligh Reef, on an island that, thanks to a westerly gale, oil never reached, I'm searching for innocence in the form of a modest speckled trout, a symbol of Prince William Sound as it was before the disaster—unblemished, wild, without scars. The salmon I've found by the thousands are a good sign; life in six-pound packages, spawning, dying, and proliferating—proof that every act of destruction (or, in the case of spawning salmon, self-sacrifice) is in one way or another an act of creation.

The morning is uncharacteristically dry for a region notoriously wet, prone to snotty Gulf Coast squalls blowing rain and fog. A half mile from the tidal flats, my stream pours from a tunnel of moss-bearded conifers—hemlock and Sitka spruce (the "Cadillac of structural woods," according to those familiar with its kiln-dried grain). The banks are edged in salmonberry tangles whose fruit, resembling flesh-colored raspberries, is sweet and as large as a man's thumb.

This, for me, is not home water, and therein, beyond my quest for mysterious little trout, lies the intrigue. I've spent the last thirty years well north of here, beyond a range of coastal mountains, in a region less temperate. So I'm learning as I go, about the land and about the fish. There will be no rainbow trout or grayling like I'm used to finding in my Susitna Valley streams. But the pink salmon are familiar. In August they're tough to get away from. And I'm expecting a Dolly Varden or two, pleasant incidentals, but beside the point.

Inside the rain forest, sunlight falls in fractured rays, projectiles of light piercing an otherwise dusky understory. A whiff of rotting fish makes me aware suddenly of the rifle slung over one shoulder. I round a bend, cautiously, and, sure enough, there on a sandbar lay a pair of mangled salmon, bellies and brains ripped out. Brown bear. Ubiquitous as pink salmon this time of year. The tracks lead in and out of the salmonberry tangles. For the rest of the day I will sound like an addled fool, talking to myself loudly, singing at the top of my lungs. The bears will know I'm coming. I don't want any surprises.

The challenge today is in finding water that isn't swarming with salmon. To cast among them is to foul-hook a hump-backed dorsal. The trout, if they're here, will hold beneath undercut banks or in pools unoccupied by snapping salmon jaws. Trouble is, there are no guarantees that the trout are here now.

Salmon begin to thin out as I make my way upstream. Less than a dozen hover in a foaming pool. My fly is a hot-pink Woolly Bugger. It looks less like fish food than something a woman might pin to her lapel for a cocktail party. I'm told by a man who fishes for these trout in Oregon that this can be an effective pattern. Of course, if I can find them, most any fly will likely work. Cutthroat trout, particularly *wild* Alaskan cutthroat trout, are reputedly easy.

When I look at a cutthroat trout, I am reminded of a shy child, freckled, cast out of the mainstream because it is small, less aggressive. (The name, cutthroat, is derived not from the creature's disposition, but from its appearance. Cutthroats lack, along their lateral lines, the decisive pink stripes of rainbow trout, wearing them instead in distilled vividness under each side of the jaw.)

In fact, Alaska's coastal cutts are particularly susceptible to bullying. When spawning, they seek tiny streams—muskeg trickles, remote headwaters, springs barely a foot wide—to avoid competition from belligerent silver salmon and steelhead.

Young fish spend three or four years in freshwater, eating gluttonously, putting on weight, gaining strength. By the time they've reached eight inches or so in length, they are ready to enter the sea. Normally they do so in May, spending anywhere from a few days to three or four months following the coastline, feeding on the ocean's bounty. They rarely wander more than forty miles from their home streams. In the shrinking days of fall, sea-going cutthroats reassemble in their natal streams where they spend the winter.

Alaska is a place where people, too, come and go with the seasons. Our commercial fishing industry is rife with transients who arrive with the salmon runs, only to fly south with fat wallets weeks later when the first traces of snow—"termination dust"— blanket distant crags. More come here from Outside seeking fortunes in oil, gold, construction, prostitution. Mostly, they take their money and leave. But a select few choose to stay on.

In a similar vein, not all coastal cutthroat trout are anadromous. In some streams they are found in both sea-run and resident forms. No one seems to know why one fish spends time in the ocean while another of the same species in the same stream does not. But then, as in all natural occurrences, the little fish likely follow profound schematics that biologists and anglers can only hope to trace. In the end, they are where you find them, one day among the barnacles chasing minnows, the next sipping mayflies from muskeg freshets.

So here I am, in Prince William Sound, on this little creek suggested to me by a biologist friend who sampled it in the years following the '89 oil spill. The place, he'd promised, supports sea-run cutts—he didn't know how many—but he'd once found some here. Timing, he told me, is the key; a slippery tip for chasing fish with such nebulous agendas.

The first pool is long and free, somehow, of salmon. Casting here is easy, since the creek is bordered by gravel bars and, amid the deep forest, backcast-snagging brush is minimal, screened out by old growth. I plop the pink Woolly Bugger into the head of the pool and am surprised to see a horde of small shadows jump on it. In seconds I'm playing a frisky eight-inch fish—about what I'd expected. Still, there is something anticlimactic about finding what I am looking for on the first try and then having it only barely fulfill minimal expectations.

I'm anticipating black spots and red jaws as I draw the little fish near, but the colors, though familiar, do not match: olive-drab back, gun-metal-blue sides, pink polka dots. Dolly Varden.

There are certain items, mostly among the gear I use for hunting and fishing, that exist in an odd sort of limbo: a folding knife I've kept since boyhood, a bag of spare fly lines, a harmonica I sometimes take on wilderness trips. These things are never quite lost. Sometimes, one or another will vanish for extended periods—a summer, a year, occasionally longer. But in time, they always turn up, out of the periphery, normally when I least expect them. Cutthroat trout possess a similar vagueness.

My first encounter with them was years ago in December, when Alaska was dark and frozen. I'd escaped to Vancouver Island, Haig-Brown country, temperate, spring-like even during winter's shortest days. I was casting for winter steelhead in the Cowichan River when I sensed a sharp pluck, then nothing. I retrieved the fly and cast again, crouching slightly, focusing.

My streamer hung briefly at the end of the drift, a bright contradiction to the off-green current, when a shadow darted in and snatched it. The struggle was desperate, but short. The fish came to hand and I was taken first by the eye: a wet, black stone set in a brass ring, staring without expression, a prelude to fourteen inches of leopard-spotted, coppery-skinned trout. In that fertile river, the fish could have been a brown, a rainbow, even a sea-run Dolly Varden. But the trout gasped as I freed the hook, and the gill plates flared, displaying broad orange stripes underneath. My first cutthroat, unmistakable, bigger than life. I held the fish in the current, then let go, watched it dissolve into the pool.

Time has a way of eroding certain milestones; some inevitably are lost. I cannot recall catching my very first grayling or Dolly Varden. But Alaskan cutthroats have come only recently; the memories are fresh, the images crisp.

Late one April, years after those brass-eyed, scarlet-jawed Cowichan River jewels, I planned a steelhead fishing trip to an island stream in southeast Alaska. The steelhead, as it turned out, were few. I hooked only two and lost them both, but I wasn't disappointed completely. While casting a #6 Rajah to a classic steelhead run, I stuck my first Alaskan cutthroat trout. Just one in four days of fishing.

The cutthroat struck with every ounce of its might, leaping out the riffles three times before I keel-hauled it in on my eight-weight rod. As with its Canadian cousins, the ten-inch fish was a lovely incidental, worthy of an admiring glance. My main focus was on the big sea-run rainbows, and yet, in the back of my mind, I thought I might like to set aside time one day for cutthroats alone, so game, so colorful, so innocent. So overlooked.

Farther upstream, I've come to another pool, this one deeper, bordered on the far side by a short rock bluff and fed by a chute of frothing water the color of dark beer. A few pinks hover near the tailout, but the hole under the chute appears salmon-free. My cast, though adequate, is unspectacular, a two-strip, backhand fling.

Prince William Sound marks the northwestern edge of the cutthroat's range. Prior to 1989, most cutt streams here were known to support delicate populations of perhaps 200 trout apiece. Then came the spill, the storm, the oil lapping ashore in viscous tides.

It makes me wonder.

My fly plops into the roiling water beneath the chute, and in a heartbeat, it is seized by something that turns and runs straight downstream, making my reel buzz, causing me to fumble, shocked. I'm certain right off that the fish is not a salmon (it's big, but not *that* big); it feels, to my delight, more like a furious rainbow trout. Near the end of the run, the fish—a silvery, flashing thing—skips once, twice, three times, shaking like a wet dog.

At times like this, when I'm exploring, the last thing I want to do is lose a fish before it can be positively identified. The impetus of this trip, the key to its success or failure, hinges on finding not just any fish, but a particular kind of fish. Call it a form of trophy hunting (though I prefer to think of trout more as treasures than trophies), call it simple curiosity; I've asked a question and am dying for an answer. Flyfishing, for this one moment, has entered a phase of seriousness that is undeniable.

The fish turns at the end of the pool, scattering the gang of hulking pinks, sending them downstream, splashing through a riffle. I'm gaining line when my fish leaps twice more, then runs to the chute at the pool's head and turns and runs back down. This happens, to various extents, three more times before the fish gives in and follows the line into the shallows.

This is no snaky, head-shaking Dolly—the intense, fluttering struggle told me that. From kype to caudal, it is vaguely shy of eighteen inches long, dime-bright, with sea-lice on its flanks, marking an arrival in freshwater within the last forty-eight hours. Black flecks dapple the back and sides, and the slashes under the gills, though faint, say it all.

For an instant, I am tempted to reel up and call it a trip, since the day would be no less brilliant if it ended right here, among sweet salmonberries and sunlight shafts filtered through the rain forest, with the trackless stream chugging among stones and the sprucy, ginlike air. But I've traveled too far, waited too long. Every pool after this one, every eddy, holds cutthroat trout. They top at eighteen inches, average around twelve. Some are like the first, silver-sided, fresh from the sea; others, likely resident fish, show painted flanks the color of fireweed honey, dark, peppered with black spots, a faint purple sheen on the gill plates and shoulders. They strike without inhibition, and I reach a point (actually reach it long before I stop fishing) where the appeal of catching diminishes altogether. Something inside seems sated, soothed.

Now the afternoon fades gently, with a dusky softness unique to August evenings in Alaska. I'm walking downstream, under fluttering bats, realizing that, in their own subtle way, cutthroat trout are metaphors for Prince William Sound, and for Alaska in general: beautiful, wild, innocent. Vulnerable.

They are works of an artful creator, fragile, finite, delicate as this isolated corner of the world. They are worth finding and catching and letting go—for fun and for reassurance. The Sound, through no fault of our own, is yet alive. Today I've held the proof in my very own hands.

A Road Runs
Through It

Gray's Creek was an unlikely, out-of-the-way place for salmon fishing, narrow and brushy at its Parks Highway crossing, the water shallow, rusty. But on drizzling evenings in August, a bear-fearing angler could go there with an eight-weight rod and a large-bore rifle (a .300 H & H magnum is about right) and catch silvers—Susitna River–run fish, fresh and strong—catch them until his forearm wore out.

The secret lay in a wisp of a game trail, known only to a few locals, that traced the sphagnum along an adjacent ridge. The trail threaded for a mile or so through dense black spruce that bristled with the blond, frizzy shoulder hair of passing grizzlies, then dropped into a hollow where Gray's met the Susitna River. Here, Gray's flagged, grew wide under banks that fell abruptly into deep shadows. Often, you could hear silvers before you saw the creek, rolling, tailing, swirling, as silvers will, in the quiet water. The mouth of Gray's, though tannin, was translucent; a perfect resting place for salmon weary from fighting the Su's muddy, glacial flow.

This backwater, the only area truly fishable, was small—just right for a guy and his wife or two friends. But with the years, the game trail grew wider, more substantial, its moss bottom pounded to mud on wet nights, dust on dry. And when the time came that you could no longer count on having the place to yourself, when along the roadside below the ridge ten cars and trucks (and, once, a school bus!) might be parked, Gray's lost its magic and I stopped going there.

In its own way, Gray's could serve as a micro-study in westward expansion: a vulnerable Eden, delicate and finite, discovered and destroyed by too many sharing similar dreams. When people outnumber fish, as they often do in the accessible places these days, and when beer cans and monofilament wads outscore people, the question is as irrepressible as it is unsettling: *yes, it is good that people have an Alaska to run to, but where do we go from here?*

A windless, cloudless August day on the Copper River Delta is rare, like gold, only bigger and much brighter because it is filled with things that are alive. Things that run and fly and swim. This is a place of wetlands—rivers, sloughs, and ponds—where waterfowl nest. There are ducks and shorebirds of all types, trumpeter swans white as snow, and dusky Canada geese, a particularly small, ash-colored race of the species. Everything under the cool blue sky is a unique shade of green: sedges, willows, hemlocks, alders. Mountains rise abruptly, framing the place on three sides like a mammoth amphitheater.

This is Alaska, wild and open as it's ever been, where bald eagles nest in cottonwood tops, where wolves howl, and where brown bears grow fat on salmon. It's the last frontier in its truest sense—except for one striking fact. A road runs through it.

My past is paved with lonesome roads, narrow, deserted tracks that no longer exist, at least not in forms that I now recognize. There was the Glenn Highway of my youth, a cracked, pinched thread of asphalt snaking its way over Eureka Summit, where each fall we staged to hunt caribou in the surrounding hills. And there was the Richardson, a remote link to moose meadows and grayling streams out of Paxson; the Taylor, gravel to this day, dust-choked in July, slimy in August; the Tok Cutoff, paved, where snowshoe hares bounced across the road in numbers unbelievable, the like never seen since populations crashed sometime around the Watergate era.

Ten years ago, en route to Dawson City, Yukon, I stopped for the night at the Little Tok River. I spent a quiet evening casting dry flies to foot-long grayling, then huddled alongside a campfire later that night, breathing wood smoke and air touched by willows and spruce. While gathering dead alder for firewood, I stumbled upon a section of the old Tok Cutoff long abandoned, a stretch that, as a boy, I'd passed over many times.

The next morning I rose with the sun and started walking it. The center line had faded, the lanes were crumbling, willows sprouted knee-high. Incredibly, patches of fur and light bone dried by wind and sun marked the remains of hares, road kills fifteen years old.

I walked for several miles, bleeding from old wounds (an inevitability of time travel), renewing ties to a past suddenly confirmed, until the road ended abruptly at a washed-out bridge. In the end, the whole experience seemed oddly metaphysical, like finding a letter written by a family member long dead. That, of course, is what roads are meant for—to take you places, to show you things.

Now, in a rental van in the middle of the Copper River Flats, I am traveling another highway, one very much like those I once knew: rough, remote, virtually untraveled. Tony Route's driving, we have the day to explore, to fish, to drive this road's length to nowhere since it, too, ends abruptly at a bridge.

We'd splashed down the night before on Eyak Lake in Cordova, hungry and thirsty, returning from a trout-fishing crusade on an island stream in Prince William Sound. Cordova, a fishing town nestled on the Sound's eastern edge, is a quiet place on August nights when the salmon fleet's out working the Copper River Delta for chums and silvers. Still, the beer flowed at the Reluctant Fisherman, chasing a shot or two of Wild Turkey like ice on a burn. We enjoyed the nightlife, subdued as it was, until the dark, wee hours, then drove to a picnic and recreation site outside of town, pitching a tent by the high beams of our rental.

The plan was to return by jet to Anchorage late the next day after fishing some streams outside of Cordova. Hours later, hot sunlight piercing the tent had roused us, and by mid-morning we were rumbling in a cloud of dust along the Copper River Highway, halfway to the Million Dollar Bridge.

Thirteen miles of pavement backed by thirty-four miles of gravel, the Copper River Highway was conceived in 1908 as the proposed Copper River & Northwestern Railway. The railway was to link the port of Cordova to the rich Kennecott copper mines 196 miles north in the Wrangell Mountains. Sounded like a great idea at the time, but first someone had to figure out how to bridge the powerful Copper River.

Imagine bridging an enormous river a third of a mile wide, swift, swirling, opaque with brown glacial silt; the channel being an expressway for icebergs, some rising twenty feet above the water, calved from glaciers upstream. The current rips at a steady ten miles per hour, twenty-four hours a day, day in, day out (a river, as we know, never sleeps). Between April and July, water levels may fluctuate twenty-four feet.

For starters, you'd need a bridge that will stand well above the high-water mark, with enough clearance to allow towering icebergs to pass safely underneath. The bridge will consist of four steel spans, all fronted by knife-edged ice-breakers cast of steel and concrete to keep bridge piers from being swept out by massive ice jams. The spans will weigh approximately 4,000,000 pounds apiece, and—here's the crazy part—every last pound must be pulled with ropes at least twenty miles upriver on barges and canoes towed by men scrambling through alder tangles and over boulders ranging in size from a man's head, to the girth of a motor home.

The job seemed impossible. Yet, through a mix of genius and sheer cussedness on the parts of railway engineers and scores of laborers, the bridge (named the Million Dollar Bridge for its cost) spanning the Copper at a bottleneck between the Child's and Miles glaciers was completed in 1910. Within a year, the railway to Kennecott was complete.

Construction of the Copper River Highway as it exists today began in 1958 over the old railway bed. By 1962, the highway stretched several miles beyond the Million Dollar Bridge, still solid after more than fifty years. But just when it seemed likely that Cordova would be connected by road to the rest of the state, tragedy struck in the form of Alaska's savage 1964 earthquake.

Tsunamis—great tidal waves created by the quake's shock—swept places like Seward and Valdez. Buildings toppled in Anchorage. People were killed. And the death knell for the completion of the Copper River Highway was sounded. The highway was broken by cracks six feet deep, its bridges left twisted, sagging, and—the finishing blow—the fourth span of the great Million Dollar Bridge had collapsed. Plans to finish the highway were tabled indefinitely.

Tony and I spent the first part of the day visiting the bridge and it was awesome; we walked on it, got a little dizzy looking down at the river still tearing like a wild animal at those old piers, ready to swallow a man in a second. From there, at the sound of thunder—

the ground literally shaking—we rushed down a side spur and watched ice calve off Child's Glacier into the raging Copper. Boulders the size of truck tires lay scattered among trees fifty yards from the river, washed there by incredible waves sent by plunging walls of ice a quarter-mile high. A sign nearby warned that it is illegal to collect salmon swept ashore by calving ice. A second sign warned to beware of the eight-hundred-pound brown bears that appear from the woods to disregard sign number one.

The sightseeing portion of our tour was over. We drove south from the Million Dollar Bridge, over the gravel Copper River Highway, dodging heaps of brown bear scat the way drivers in ranch country dodge cow patties. It was time to get serious, to check out a few area waters.

A brook flowing sprightly among alders and cottonwoods seemed worth a stop, but turned out to be too narrow and shallow for casting. Down the road, a trail mashed in the grass led to water sparkling through branches and leaves. A local secret? Turned out to be a moose trail leading to a beaver pond, stagnant, mud-bottomed, showing nothing but a few sticklebacks. Dead ends are always to be expected when poking around in country you've never before fished.

The fish were there; pilots at Fishing and Flying Aviation and locals at the Reluctant Fisherman dropped names like Power Creek (Dollys), Alaganik Slough (cutthroats), and McKinley Lake among several other streams and lakes with more informal names like "Nine-mile" and the "Second-Culvert-Past-the-Airport." All we had to do was find fishable water.

The best fishing along Alaska's highways seems to have gone largely the way of the Susitna Valley's Gray's Creek. That's partly because our highway system is limited—roughly 2,750 miles serving 586,412 square miles or a one-mile strip for every 213 square miles. More than a million visitors toured Alaska between May 1996 and April 1997. Add to that a resident population of 600,000, the majority of whom live along the road system, and you come up with more than 600 people (and scores of potential roadside anglers) per highway mile. From the perspective of whitewalls and asphalt, this immense, "untamed wilderness" state can seem suddenly crowded.

The stream comes as a surprise, a fountain of questions so natural and active that it seems alive, as if its source might be traced to a great heart, ancient, throbbing. There are no road signs, nothing about the road that seems especially fishy, just a dusty spur parting from the main highway toward the coastal mountains. The sun is high, about two o'clock, orbited by an immature bald eagle that hangs from unflapping wings. Our plane home isn't scheduled to leave until 6:30 this evening, so Tony pulls off, and within 200 yards, the spur ends on the bank of this stream flanked by willow and tall grass.

No wider than a firm, comfortable cast, the main run flows at a brisk walking pace, thigh-deep, gravel-bottomed, pocked with pools deeper than an average man stands tall. The water is cold, the color of vodka and ice, absolutely transparent.

Sometimes I think about the changes that have come to Alaska within my lifetime, seeing myself as a sort of island, innocent, unaltered. But I have changed. Standing on the bank of this gorgeous stream, my thoughts are tainted by suspicion: *where are the people?* Tony and I discuss the possibilities. The stream might be closed to fishing. Perhaps there are no fish. These are the questions of cynics too far removed from a time when such finds were accepted as matters of course. There is a certain sadness in that. But at the moment, with the stream pouring its heart out and fly rods in the van, there is no time for looking back.

It is good on this hot day to wade into the icy stream past my knees, feeling its coolness as a flyfisher should, just right through thick neoprene. Casting will be easy, though choosing a first fly, as always in unfamiliar water, is a challenge.

A scarlet cloud—red salmon—ten feet long, six feet wide, hovering in a seam midstream makes my decision for me. Behind them I can expect to find scavengers, Dolly Varden or cutthroat trout, following like wolves, waiting for those eggs to drop. I tie on an Iliamna Pinkie, a perfectly crafted chenille salmon egg, and in a moment, I'm casting.

The first couple of drifts pass over the salmon that, in water so clear, turn out to be holding deeper than I thought. I strip out more line, falsecast to pick my spot, and drop the fly, preceded by a split shot, ten feet upstream. In a moment, the little pink spot vanishes under the bellies of undulating salmon, a few of which remain sea-bright. I'm prepared for the jolt that follows; the salmon part and a chrome flash tears up the center. I'm holding on, shouting to Tony that I've hooked a fresh red.

I wonder occasionally if my choice of tackle is driven not as much by a yen for sport as it is by a sort of calculated pessimism, since often, thinking small, I find myself undergunned by fish too large for lightweight rods. My four-weight is bowed radically, pulsing, the drag squealing on my reel. Tony's behind me on the bank, rigging up, watching closely. The fish turns before it reaches my backing, then screams downstream, leaving me reeling madly to catch up. For an instant, the line goes slack, so I reef back on the rod, feel a thump, an instant of tension. The fish wallows frantically on the surface, not like a salmon, showing off thick shoulders, and then the fly pulls out, the fish is gone.

I turn to Tony, my heart beating still to the rhythm of the struggle. Tony is lighting his pipe and for a moment there is silence. Then, through a puff of white smoke, he speaks, "Hell of a Dolly." And suddenly, it all makes sense—the chrome flash, the head-shaking wallow.

Our stream has more surprises. I'm standing there in mid-channel, discussing with Tony the possibilities implicit in hooking fish so big so quickly, when something splashes in a pool between us. It's as if an unseen bird dropped a small stone. The conversation stops as we watch, curious.

Alaskan salmon streams, where trout and char key on spawn and flesh, can be deceptive. The last thing we expect to see, particularly here in the Copper River Flats behind a knot of red salmon, are fish rising. But there it was again, a splashing, swirling riseform. Unmistakable. Tony has already tied on his own Pinkie, and figuring whatever it is might be hungry for eggs as well as bugs, we both start casting. In seconds we're catching grayling—fish not known by biologists nor anyone else to frequent streams in this area.

The grayling play well on our light rods, and we're glad to have them. The state stocks grayling in a couple of local lakes, including one that we were unable to find on the flats near the highway. Perhaps a bucket biologist caught a few and dumped them in this creek. Or maybe in spring floods some escaped and ended up here.

Within a few hours we've worked up and down the stream, catching more grayling, Dollys to three pounds, and a couple of red salmon that make our hearts jump, our reels scream. Bear trails and the rotting corpses of half-eaten salmon lend the day a distinct wilderness feel. Yet just beyond those willows upstream, our van waits, on a road, just off the historic Copper River Highway. And something about that feels good, makes me realize that Alaska is, after all, a big place; that maybe a guy with a little imagination *can* go home again.

We showed up at the airport that evening with our duffels and fly rods, a little grimy, smelling faintly of the fish we'd released back to that clear, cold stream. We left wanting more.

Since the '64 quake, talk about reviving construction of the Copper River Highway continues, building every few years to an angry head. Cordova today is divided by those who want the link and those who prefer to keep life simple and isolated. It all makes a person wonder—about "progress," westward expansion, and lessons learned too late at little out-of-the-way places. Places like Gray's Creek.

Bloody Knuckles

I am ready for a fight, focused, muscles taut; I've got that tickling feeling in my chest, a slight weakness in the knees. I haven't come unarmed. My weapons are ugly, intimidating—a Sage ten-weight, thick, heavy enough to knock out a black bear; a stout Ross reel; a leader like towing cable. This is a hunt for big game; no messing around.

Flyfishing sometimes comes off, rightly, as a marriage of sport and art, a sensual melding of action, vision, physics, and philosophy. It becomes a kind of self-expression, an extension of ourselves as we imitate form, color, movement, and other elements of nature. This may explain, perhaps, why there are as many reasons to stand thigh-deep in ice water waving a stick as there are moods and flyfishers.

But today is different. I'm here for reasons predating art and sport, reasons more basic, primal.

I'm standing at the mouth of a Kahiltna River tributary, a tannic freestone stream mixing into the Kahiltna's glacial flow like coffee into cream. Out front, fish the size of Angus calves roll in the dark water. King salmon.

I am drawn to king salmon by their awesomeness. They are big, strong, *manly* fish, and the temptation is to blame their allure on testosterone or insecurities brought on by too many John Wayne flicks as a kid. (The Duke: *"I'm not gonna punch ya ... like hell I'm not!"*) But that's too easy. Besides, I occasionally find myself equally intrigued by foot-long trout.

Still, here on the river, I can't deny a certain urgency, a need to go one-on-one, to prove by landing one of these fish something I can't quite explain. It needles me.

The fly is an out-sized #3/0 Battle Creek Special, the pink-and-white egg-cluster imitator that's so deadly in smaller dimensions on trout, char, and silver salmon. The hook is heavy, galvanized and the fly casts like a stone. I can see salmon hovering midstream, a couple of dozen, stacked like nervous torpedoes.

My first casts are accompanied by a sense of mild desperation, fishing's equivalent of buck fever. I'm forced to remind myself that there is no hurry, the salmon are holding, resting from days of blind struggle up the silty Susitna River and the merging Kahiltna. Better to try and enjoy the day, perhaps eighty degrees, baking-hot for Alaska; my forearms are turning pink, like the wild roses blooming along the far bank.

Soon I'm settled in, dropping my fly upstream of the salmon, letting it sink to the gravel that massages their white bellies. The pattern is familiar: cast, drift, pause, nothing. Cast, drift, pause … like playing a one-armed bandit, waiting for the jackpot. It's a monotonous game, hypnotic, mindless.

So my thoughts are far away when it happens. The strike is abrupt, brutal. It surges through my arms, neck, and shoulders like lightning. There's no time to react, to set the hook, before the salmon runs, scattering the rest of the pod, splitting the run with a boiling wake. Everything's happening too fast; my impulse is to slam on the brakes, palm the reel, gain control. The reel handle spins frantically, beating my palm. I clamp down and my rod jolts forward instantly, as if I've snagged a passing bus; then there's a pop and the reel stops spinning. The tension is gone.

My heart pounds, my legs tremble with unspent adrenaline. Art and form have gone suddenly out the window. The message is clear. The heart of king salmon fishing is in the struggle, the powerful out-and-out brawl of it.

Thirty minutes later I'm casting again, same pattern, better leader, still kicking myself for fumbling that first chance. I'm wide awake, sharp, measuring the current's pull, feeling the tap-tap-tap of my fly over every stone in the river. This time I'm ready.

When it comes finally, the strike is as bone-jarring as the first. I strike back, as wickedly and powerfully as I can, reminding me of a bar fight years ago at the Sawmill Club in Anchorage. A surly drunk had spit in a friend's face and on reflex I'd punched him in the eye. On television a jab like that sends bad guys on their cans. But that night at the bar had been real life.

My fingers still grip the line as the salmon takes off, running, thrashing, leaping. Pain—searing, intense—forces me to let go and the reel again spins out of control. From here on the details get hazy; I'm acting and reacting impulsively, too intent on the struggle to take notes.

When the dust settled that night at the Sawmill Club, the drunk had broken away and lurched off through the gloom. My friend and I also left, before the cops arrived. I was grinning insanely, nursing a shoulder that I discovered later was dislocated.

Now, on the river, my biceps and shoulders ache. I kneel to pull the hook from the king salmon, a forty-pounder, easy; then watch it sidle away, panting heavily through pumping gills, its thick, muscle-bound back parting the shallows. My palm is bruised from the screaming reel, and blood from the cuts the line left on my thumb and forefinger drips into the amber water and turns purple.

I'm not much for bar fights these days, but there's no denying a need to in some way challenge, compete, go head-to-head against another power source as a way to better define myself, my place in the world. That's probably a dangerous admission in this age of battered masculinity, where anything male seems fair game for attack. But in my heart, I know that it's okay to be a man, to pursue "manly" things. The rush that I felt then and now, a sort of manic exhilaration, is one that men in the wake of battle have likely always known.

At the moment, I'm feeling a little worn-out, ragged. But guys like me don't give up that easily. In a minute, I'm picking myself up from the gravel, wiping my bloody hand on my shirt, and wading out for another round.

Thomas McGuane (whom I don't know personally, but whose writing I admire) says that everyone in Montana acquires, as a birthright, a knowledge of horses, whether or not they have ever owned or ridden one. The same could be said of Alaskans and king salmon.

Most school kids know that kings are the state fish, the largest of five species of Pacific salmon, the first to run each spring. The current state sport record is 97 lbs. 4 oz., a fish heaved with considerable effort from the Kenai River in 1985. Yet there have been, and likely remain, bigger. Alaska's largest known king salmon, caught decades ago in a Petersburg fish trap, weighed 126 pounds.

Kings enter streams from May to August, with runs peaking generally in June or early July, depending upon the region. They are strong and agile, fish of remarkable stamina. One particularly tough race bound for spawning gravel in the Yukon River headwaters traverses Alaska's complete width, struggling more than 2,000 river miles in sixty days to procreate in Canada.

Rumor has it that connoisseurs of king salmon as table fare can sample a forkful of fresh-broiled fillet, chase it with a shot of wine, and announce with incredible accuracy the origin of the fish. This can be explained by differences in texture, flavor, and fat content—the result of salmon in individual drainages adapting to their own distinct spawning hurdles. The finest-eating salmon come from the fisheries of the Yukon and Copper rivers, where fish, adapted for long, difficult runs, sport decidedly more fat and oil to carry them through their freshwater travels. Salmon whose spawning grounds wait closer to the sea tend to be proportionately leaner, drier to the taste, coarser.

As with all Pacific salmon, whose energies are fuses that begin burning the minute they leave saltwater, king salmon are best caught early on. Roderick Haig-Brown, who fished for them in British Columbia, wrote that kings are best "for only a week or two after the run begins. Maturity comes rapidly, and the fish turn sulky and slow. They have strength and weight, but no zip." This is also true of Alaskan king salmon.

Sea-bright king salmon are dynamos. Though inclined to run deep and bulldog stubbornly, fresh fish often will leap a time or two when hooked, stopping anglers' hearts. One summer day in 1993, when more than 45,000 king salmon entered the Kenai River, a pair of drift anglers were shocked when a thirty-five-pound king leapt into their boat. The local newspaper reported that the fish hit one man in the back, fell flopping on the seat of the boat, then rolled back into the river, never to be seen again.

The king salmon's soul lies in its great size and its determination to persevere against all odds. We catch them where we can: in the green waters of the Kenai River, the slate-gray salt near Ketchikan, the black water Susitna Valley streams. Each fishery, in synergy with its distinct environment, lends dimension to a revered fish.

I have a confession. In my darker moments, I have considered king salmon a bane, because they are so incredibly popular and because of the undeniable greed they inspire. Kings are deliciously marketable, a blend of power, drama, girth, mystique; they spawn hype in blasphemous degrees.

The television and radio spots each summer are relentless: "The kings are in!" Blah-blah-blah. "The *mighty* chinook!" Blah-blah-blah. "C'mon, let's go fishing!" Local newspapers print the latest on where to go and how to catch 'em. Guide boats clog the Kasilof, the lower Kenai River, the Deshka (when enough kings appear there to allow fishing—mysteriously poor returns have closed the river to king salmon fishing in recent years).

The obscenity of these crowds is defined by the litter left in their wakes. Toilet paper; disposable diapers; feces, fly-blown, fouling the air; liquor bottles; beer cans; monofilament wads. The sadness is unavoidable along the smaller streams of the Parks Highway—Willow, Montana, Goose creeks—even fly-in places like the mouth of Friday Creek on the Talachulitna River.

This is as difficult to admit as it is to read; those with axes to grind, who make their livings on the blood of these great salmon, will be angry. But take a riverboat ride upstream from Talkeetna in late June and look around the mouth of Clear Creek. Try to get out of earshot of boom-boxes and elbow-to-elbow mobs at Crooked Creek on the Kasilof or even at Saylor's Pit on the Gulkana when the kings are running.

These places have lost something. Fortunately, in the scheme of this massive state, they are exceptions—accessible, fulfilling certain human and economic needs that are on one hand important, but on the other, suspect and contrary to the whole point of fishing. And caught in the middle of it all are the king salmon, which, like Alaska, belong to no one and to everyone. In many ways the big kings are perfect Alaskan icons, up for grabs, fitting symbols of shameless exploitation, the last, best fish of the last, best place.

At 2 A.M., with the moon just forty-eight hours shy of full, the Karluk River valley can be a fearsome place. Wispy clouds, black and blue, pass over the moon's fat, yellow face; weird creatures (foxes probably, but who knows?) shriek down by the river. Willows shining in the silver light become wicked apparitions. Everything seems unreal.

I'm huddled on a knoll overlooking camp, fiddling nervously with a .45-caliber revolver—it might as well be a squirt gun. Nearby, David Hagen stares into the night, clutching a 12-gauge Model 97. Our hearts pound audibly, *ka-thunk-ka-thunk-ka-thunk*, like troubled spirit drums.

Earlier, David had wheeled and shouted, *"Bear! Bear!"* Galloping over the soft tundra, almost on top of us, a heavy creature big as a quarter horse had flared and plunged into a thicket of willows. Guns drawn, we had scanned the darkness with our headlamps and, amid popping brush, spotted green eyes glowering back at us.

So now we're shivering in the middle of the night, watching our camp a hundred yards below, the two of us resembling, I imagine, unlikely caricatures of Custer's Last Stand. All we can do is wait for dawn.

Up until a couple of hours ago, the day had been magnificent. David and I, along with David's father, Larry, and David's teenage cousin, Devon, had spent three days rafting the Karluk River from its source at Karluk Lake.

Kodiak Island in late June is an enormous Zen garden. Almost everything, from the river's treeless banks to the flanking mountains, is verdant, vibrant, pulsing green. Lupines, Jacob's Ladder, and mountain geraniums in lush, knee-high groves appear as moody-blue islands in a rolling green sea, and the atmosphere is rich, serene, pastoral in a feral sense, with blacktail deer and rooting brown bears replacing cattle.

Running through the center of it all is the Karluk, a gentle stream, shallow, narrow enough in most places to cross with a firm cast. We'd been told that, if you don't stop to fool around, the passage from Karluk Lake to the sea requires only eighteen hours. The pace had been pleasant. We'd planned five days, which made fooling around a priority.

The lake outlet had boiled with red salmon—230,000 come up the river, according to Alaska Department of Fish and Game counts—some spawning, others fresh. We'd worn ourselves out taking them on Sockeye Orange wet flies, tinsel-bodied patterns with fiery hackles and black calftail wings. Sporadic hatches of big Green Drakes (easily #8s) fluttered over the river, and with floating lines and dry flies, we'd caught Dollys to three pounds and young steelhead, "half-pounders," fourteen- to eighteen-inches long.

But something had been missing, if only in a subliminal sense, until the third evening. Upstream from a group of cabins at Larson Bay Portage, we'd drifted around a bend on the tail of a squall that was brief but earnest, when someone saw a king salmon roll. Minutes later another broad, silver back broke the surface, and then another. Soon, big, sea-fresh kings were scooting beneath the raft.

The cabins were occupied by some Frenchmen (who marked their presence with their national flag) and a group of tweedy Italians wading the river gripping double-fisted Spey rods at least twelve feet long. The men formed a loose gauntlet for a few hundred yards, a dozen or so casting flies into eddies where big dorsals porpoised. We passed through and several of the men waved and smiled in the international language of anglers enjoying the time of their lives.

When people take the time and expense to reach places as remote as the Karluk River, the defining moments of the trip, beyond catching fish, often center on savoring a sense of aloneness. Most anglers feel this way and allow themselves and others a certain meditative space where they can fill their lungs and cast their lines without distraction. So we continued on, past the happy Europeans, beyond the glut of king salmon tailing below the cabins, knowing that rivers are continuums and the current has a way of spreading things out.

Hours later, at the verge of a canyon five miles inland from the sea, we pulled up on a grassy flat and called it a day. A steady rain fell, and hours of passively riding the current had left us chilled and hungry. By the time our tents were up and dinner served, it was too late to fish. Still, before I turned in, I stood in the drizzle at the river's edge, watching. Upstream, two truck-sized boulders cut the current mid-channel, forming deep slicks. Holding water. After five miles of fighting the canyon's shallow whitewater, the kings would stack up there.

Inevitably, the impetus of our trip had shifted sometime around our passing of Larson Bay Portage; pick-up time was only two days off and fishing suddenly seemed more serious. King salmon in Alaska are considered big game, representing sport in its highest, rough-and-tumble form. But beyond that, they are food—solid, rich, and toothsome. The possession limit was two apiece, and from that point on, the biggest fish would be killed, gutted, and stacked in Larry's cooler to take home and freeze. Months later, during the first snows of late October or in January's frozen darkness, those great fillets—thick, orange, sweet pieces of the Karluk River as we'd found it in late June—would be shared with family and friends.

The next morning I rose early. I'd lain awake much of the night like an anxious child, listening to king salmon rolling and splashing in the lee of those boulders. The rain had stopped, leaving in its wake a silent, pale fog. I crawled out of the tent, stood in the wet grass, among chocolate lilies and Indian paintbrush, yellow and blazing like ankle-high flares. The river purled by, dark, wild, inviting, a perfect complement to a morning that was damp and cool. As the others stirred in the tents, I strung up my heaviest stick, an old fiberglass Fenwick two sizes too light for thirty-, forty-pound salmon.

After landing us on Karluk Lake, Kodiak pilot Butch Tovson had mentioned that the magic color for Karluk River kings was green. So I tied on a Green Screamer, a chartreuse rabbit-fur leech with a sprig of Krystal Flash tied on top, and walked upstream to the boulders.

The essence of flyfishing is in the anticipation, the planning, the visualizing of that moment of climax marked by the take, and the handling of the struggle that follows. My pulse quickened as I peeled off line for that first cast; in my ears I heard a strange roaring, like rolling drums announcing a big event. My streamer plopped into the still water behind one of the boulders; the outside current caught my floating line and formed a belly. Before I could straighten it out, I felt a solid tug.

Playing fourteen-inch trout or char is like fencing, a lively, bouncing one-handed affair. King salmon are different. The feeling is like arm-wrestling a desperate giant, it's you against an unforgiving dynamic, a force that taxes at once your body and your resolve.

As I'd suspected, my rod lacked the proper spine for king-sized fish—a good, stiff ten-weight (or one of those double-fisted Spey rods) would have provided more leverage and required less muscle. Fortunately, the salmon refused to leave the deep hole, alternately making short runs that burned my fingers and pausing to sulk in the seam at the current's edge. I could not afford the fish too much rest, so whenever the action stalled, I would get things moving again by reefing back on the rod the way a rider spurs a horse.

I have no idea how long I played that first king, perhaps twenty minutes—long enough to wear out my forearms. By the time the salmon began to flag, wallowing on its side in the shallows, my friends had appeared with a landing net and rods of their own. Larry scooped up my salmon, a husky thirty-pounder, and finally my shoulders relaxed, quivering.

Evening. We'd finished up dinner, rice steaming-hot with teriyaki red salmon (compliments of a mint-bright sockeye that had, somewhat out of the species' character, grabbed a Green Screamer among the king salmon). My body ached as it used to in my youth, when I worked as a private logger in the Susitna Valley, the muscles in my neck and shoulders burning with light fever fed by a passion unsated by twelve hours of casting flies to enormous salmon.

I'd never seen king salmon fishing as fast as that we enjoyed that morning. We'd all kept limits (business first), then spent hours fishing purely for that surge of adrenaline that makes sparks fly in the heart, the thrill that comes with tackling fish that are unusually big and strong. The cooler was full, weighing a hundred pounds or so. David had grabbed one end and I the other, to lift it and walk as far from camp as the meadow we'd camped in would allow—a piddling stone's throw. We were gambling, of course, against nature in a land of 3,000 stream-walking, salmon-eating brown bears.

During dinner we'd heard pistol shots upriver. Later, two men and their young boys appeared on the hill above us. They had fired the shots in the air, then stepped aside as a brown bear sow and her adolescent cubs waded into camp and helped themselves to the grub—every last crumb.

"Just thought we'd warn you," said one man, who wore a .44 on his hip, "they're on their way down. You're next."

Bears are part of living in Alaska and an element of risk you learn to live with and possibly, in a strange way, even enjoy. A paw print in the mud makes you think and keeps you sharp and, maybe because of that, you tend to notice more about everything around you. But Kodiak biologists report concentrations of more than ten bears per square mile along the Karluk River when salmon runs peak. With numbers like that, the odds of adventure are less implied than ensured.

The guy with the .44 told us his party had two days until pick-up. That's a long time to go without food, especially when you're traveling with two young boys. Larry dug into our cooler, handed the men what we could spare.

A couple hours later, after we all had turned in for the night, I found myself standing in my longjohns next to the tent with perhaps five paces of thin night air between me and an eight-hundred-pound brown bear sow and her clowning seventy-pound twin cubs. David, also clad in longjohns, was holding the shotgun in a defensive posture, as if it were fitted with a bayonet and he might reach out and jab the sow in the eye.

The bears ignored our shouts and the cubs had me spooked, wrestling in the grass virtually at our feet. I wondered what our options might be, there in the middle of a wilderness without trees. We were way too close.

Backing off, with David on the shotgun, I fired the pistol in the air three times. The bears, batting the cooler with mud-caked, hairy paws, seemed deaf. I turned to the other tent and saw Larry and Devon. Larry, more annoyed than frightened, shouted at the bears. Devon, thrilled, was hiking up his jeans with one hand, winding his camera with the other.

Desperately trying to put something between us and the bears, David and I cowered behind the raft. Then David fired the shotgun over the sow, over that head big and blocky as a pony keg, and for once she flinched, then pinned back her ears. It was an ugly moment. Synapses popped. Hearts raced. I was ready for a reckless, last-ditch shoot-out when the sow suddenly picked up that heavy cooler in her jaws and, with cubs boxing and tumbling behind, disappeared into the willows.

So now David and I are here on the hill, guarding camp under the summer moon, over a river of dreams where huge salmon roll and every sound is an approaching bear. It will be a long night, but exciting, even entertaining in a terrifying sort of way.

Tomorrow morning we'll start from scratch. The bears will sleep and we'll be off downriver, where more king salmon wait. They are awesome fish, worth pursuing and fighting for and eating. Anyone who's ever caught them will tell you that. And after all, 3,000 Kodiak brown bears can't be wrong.

Goldenfins

*But when you go back to a place where you spent
many hours of childhood, you find that some of it has
become important, if not actually numinous ...*
                                    —Thomas McGuane
                                Casting on a Sea of Memories

Listen. It is true what the older folks say, that the years flow quickly and that the world changes faster, faster on the heels of each transient day. Our hearts become stones, the passing days rivers, and when the sun sets finally, we've nothing left but our own fading reflections. I realize this now because I'm standing on the divide, in the middle of my journey, and can see the horizons of both past and future. This is an important moment.

So why am I niggled by a tiny char with yellow-orange fins?

It started recently with a recurring vision—of an idyllic composite of rock and sunlight and thin, high mountain air—the imprinted image of a distant, but real, place. I've traveled there only once, nearly killing myself along the way, stalking a Dall ram that had fled far into the peaks, over a crest of impossible crags. Got myself into a cliff-hanging situation where backing down seemed out of the question. I felt my heart drum faster, my lungs ache for breath. But finally, I'd reached the spine of a knife-edged ridge, where I paused, panting, searching for a safe way down.

The view was awesome. From my perch 4,000 vertical feet

above sea level, the Chugach Range tumbled away below me, a tossing ocean of rock, ice, and broken-tooth spires. On the ridge's far side, a sheer quarter-mile down, a chute of shale and scree fanned into an abysmal cirque filled with water the color of turquoise and cobalt—vivid, chemical-like blues. The cirque headed a box canyon that leveled into a narrow bottom of heath and scattered boulders. A sparkling thread drained the lake and wound into another blue tarn, which in turn trickled off into yet another. Lovely, I thought. That canyon would be my stairway out of the mountains.

I slung my rifle over my back and prepared to start down, when I noticed something odd about the water below. The August sun shone broadly, the day windless, yet the lake's surface seemed strangely troubled. I unslung my rifle, brought up the scope and there they were—rings, as if a group of unseen boys was down there tossing stones. I twisted up the power on my scope and took a closer look. And then I realized what I was seeing. The lake was alive with cruising shadows. *Goldenfins*. Red-bellied, resident Dolly Varden; Alaska's answer to high-country brook trout.

That afternoon, as I descended among those little mountain lakes (the largest hardly bigger than a hockey rink), coveys of rock ptarmigan clucking from boulders around me, I discovered a sanctuary of tundra and lichen, of short, sparse arctic grasses and unfished water. Goldenfins broke the lake surfaces gently, fiery bellies flashing, and I vowed to return someday with a fly rod, perhaps a three-weight, a box of dry flies (diminutive Adamses—say, #18—and Humpys, maybe a few Black Gnats), and some light leader, thin as hair.

Goldenfins. They are mysterious, enchanting little fish, resident dwarves of southcentral Alaska's mountain lakes and streams, exquisitely colored with pink-spotted flanks, orange fins highlighted by white-striped leading edges, and bellies red as arctic sunsets. They've power in those colors—variegated extractions of the Chugachs in peak autumn brilliance—and in the high, far-off places they live. For we few who've known them, they have a magic that shines.

I caught them first in Turnagain Pass, mid-1960s, as a small boy crouched on a weathered bridge at the foot of Summit Lake. The Seward Highway—today's fast track to world-famous Kenai Peninsula fishing—was then a silent, lonely ribbon of cracked asphalt threading through stunted alpine spruce and willows. Beneath the bridge, six- and eight-inch char, scores of them lined up side-by-side in long regimental rows, hovered over the outlet stream's pebbled bottom. A spinning rod rested on the bridge's gray planks, its single hook baited with a strip of flesh cut with a jackknife from the side of a fish. Boys raised in southcentral Alaska know that goldenfins are like piranhas. They crave fresh meat.

Goldenfins are protein-hungry and inherently small (catch one a foot long and you've caught a trophy) because their high-altitude sanctuaries offer little to eat, and growing seasons there are short—figure *maybe* eighty days per year of ice-free water. Really, it is a wonder that cold-blooded creatures can exist at all under such conditions. But these are tough, willful, extraordinary fish. They turn up in the damnedest places.

Two summers ago, my friend David Hagen, who shares with me an appreciation of mountain solitude and stubby, high-country char, came puffing in from a remote climb. Looking rangy and gaunt, David was pleased to report his discovery of another craggy gem full of darting goldenfins. He described a particularly isolated pond, completely landlocked, connected to nothing, yet dimpled by many fish feeding. I found the vision both pleasing and curious.

"How do you suppose those fish ever got there?" I'd asked.

David hesitated as if the question hadn't occurred to him, then answered in his quiet, shoulder-shrugging way, "Maybe God just put them there a long, long time ago."

And why not? What truly matters is that such living jewels remain in Alaska's enchanted places, and that somewhere over the course of my life, they've become part of an equation (as have the smoked-salmon smell of willow smudges on buggy July evenings, the choking dryness of glacial silt whirling in Matanuska breezes, the sweetness of moose backstraps fried in butter on damp September afternoons ...), the sum of which is me.

Until lately, goldenfins have remained out of sight, I suppose, far off in the back of my mind, only to appear suddenly, in hindsight, crisp and bright as good wine, better perhaps than they've ever been. Yet my rediscovery of them has inspired a troubling desperation—that "niggling" mentioned before—something Hemingway described as "a death loneliness that comes at the end of every day that is wasted in your life."

Truth is, I've spent too many days not casting flies to pretty little fish. Who hasn't? But that's about to change. Somewhere high in the Chugachs, secluded in a narrow box canyon, waits a chain of small lakes known only to Dall rams, rock ptarmigan, a race of minute, pink-spotted char, and me.

Alaska's Fish

David Hagen had a plan. He had keys to a friend's cabin in Moose Pass, deep in the heart of the Kenai Mountains. I'd visited the cabin before, situated at the base of a steep, three-thousand-foot, alder-covered ridge topped by an alpine saddle where mountain goats fed. Beyond that saddle, David said, was some good country: a wide tundra flat with lakes, willow-edged and dimpled by feeding goldenfin char. Ptarmigan everywhere. The time was late August—ptarmigan season—so why not tote our shotguns up there, have a nice hike over the treeless heather, and hunt some birds?

We drove up Friday evening after work with our wives and young children. Before dark, David and I hunted up some spruce grouse in the valley, under that hulking mountain range. We watched a cloud bank move in from the south, and as the evening grew darker and the air wetter, that long climb through the alders began to look dismal.

Next morning, the mountain tops were hidden in fog. The temperature sulked in the forties, and rain seemed imminent in the valley. In the high country, wet snow was a distinct possibility. I think David was still game to go—he's of Norwegian descent, long-legged, tough. But he's spent as much time climbing through wet grass and brush as I have. We'd both brought fly rods (never leave home without 'em, May through September), so when I suggested we drop our guns and head for Quartz Creek, a fifteen-minute drive away and chock-full of Dolly Varden (fat, salmon-egg-eaters to five pounds or better), David took one last look at the ridge and headed for the car. Funny how guys who aren't getting younger, who've spent decades climbing mountains in the rain, can rationalize.

Dolly Varden are silver flashes in the riffles of Tongass steelhead streams, olive-backed shadows lurking in Bristol Bay rivers, phantom dimples in high mountain lakes. No matter where you travel in Alaska, chances are that Dollys in one form or another wait close by. They are survivors, opportunists, chameleons. But more than anything else, Dolly Varden are pioneers. And in that sense, they are Alaska's fish.

My first Dollys were the goldenfins in Turnagain Pass, caught with spinning rod and bait. As I grew with the years and began flyfishing, the fish I pursued seemed to grow, too. I caught sea-run Dollys in drizzling saltwater bays, firm, dime-bright desperadoes to two, three pounds. And I caught far larger strains in streams and lakes from the Brooks Range in August, from Bristol Bay in October, and from Prince of Wales Island in April. When nothing else is happening, I can almost always count on catching Dolly Varden.

So now I'm crouching at Quartz Creek's edge, peeking through the stunted spruces and wrist-thick alders of a grown-over beaver meadow. My eyes are locked on a long green silhouette hovering behind a knot of red salmon. The question is, as always: *Which fly?* A winter at the vise preparing for such moments has provided many choices.

Something's splashing upstream, and I can see David standing among willows armpit-high, playing a heavy fish. He's gone with the obvious—Iliamna Pinkie, a salmon-egg imitation formed by a couple wraps of chenille over a short-shanked hook. It's deadly on egg-sucking Dollys.

Fair enough. In a moment, I've also tied on a Pinkie and am

casting to that long green shadow. I'm all tensed up, waiting for the take. The tiny ball of pink yarn is bouncing over pebbles, right under the Dolly's nose. No dice. The fish dodges slightly, allowing my counterfeit salmon egg to pass by. Such rejection is unheard of.

In a moment, my line is gathered up and tossed out for another pass. This time, when my fly is almost within striking distance, the fish spooks, darts out of its lie into the darker, deeper water in mid-channel. Trouble.

Alaska has changed since those innocent days when I caught red-bellied goldenfins on single hooks baited with fish-gut strips. Back then, Dolly Varden were considered by many to be nuisances: vulgar, common, gluttonous eaters of young salmon and salmon eggs. They were suitable only for dog food and for bait-fishing little boys and, not long before my time, they had a price on their tails.

To preserve commercial fishing interests, Alaska's territorial government paid a bounty of two-and-a-half cents per caudal. Tails were sun-dried or smoked, strung forty at a time on baling-wire hoops, and were used in lieu of cash in some parts of Alaska. Of course, the bounty program had its flaws.

Frank Dufresne, writer and former territorial Game Commissioner, reported in a 1963 issue of *Field & Stream*, "A sample hoop of forty tails contained fourteen rainbows, five whitefish, six lake trout, two pike, two grayling, one sucker, seven fingerling salmon, and three Dollys. Another hoop was almost all immature sockeye salmon, the very species the bounty was being paid to save!"

Fortunately, the ubiquitous Dollys refused to be misunderstood. With no other choice, we fished over them, ate them, and secretly blessed them and their willingness to strike on days when we would otherwise have gone fishless. The bounty program eventually was discontinued, and somewhere along the line, a bond developed between anglers and Dolly Varden. We discovered that prevalence is no basis for distaste. And beyond that, we realized that Dollys can grow big—fifteen pounds or better—and that they can fight like bulls. Their beauty is unquestionable, with those pink spots rising over gun-metal-blue flanks.

So finally, within the last decade, we've opened our eyes to find in Dolly Varden everything that makes a sport fish great. All of which is at the heart of my problem today. Quartz Creek, like Dolly fishing in general, was "discovered" in the late 1980s. Cars filled the Quartz Creek campground when David and I pulled up, and anglers wearing Raybans and waving expensive sticks stalked the banks all the way down to Kenai Lake. Fish that hadn't been clubbed and creeled (catch-and-release fishing for these ubiquitous char has only recently dawned on many anglers) likely had tender mouths. So David and I had busted brush to fish upstream, away from the crowds and ragged-lipped fish.

Still, I'm wondering. I reel in and sit down on the bank to go through my fly box. A smattering of raindrops, cold as the August breeze, lights on my cheeks, makes my nose tickle. Even from here, I can see that saddle in the distance, sulking in the fog. Wonder what the goldenfins are feeding on today. No sore mouths up there. I'd bet on it.

Fish for them long enough, in enough places under various conditions, and you will learn that Dolly Varden are creatures of uncommon dimension. Their appetites transcend the seasonal and geographical limits of salmon life cycles, and sometimes, in the tradition of Lower Forty-eight brook trout and spring creek browns, they become great stalkers of bugs.

On that June trip to the Karluk with David, his father Larry, and his cousin Devon, most of the early run of reds had reached the headwater lake, where they kept us awake our first night, thousands of them splashing and rolling in the shallows. The next day, as we floated downstream, sockeyes became scarce and we watched for pockets of salmon holding in slow water.

At one point, David spotted fish porpoising in a black pool at the foot of a riffle, and we pulled onto a sandbar. We stepped up to the pool confidently, with sparse sockeye streamers and sturdy rods, ready for action. Surface glare and deep water made seeing fish impossible, yet they continued rolling in front of our eyes, so we spent an hour tormenting them with Comets and Sockeye Johns, with absolutely no luck.

Rejection is the bane of we who fish. It is inescapable, inevitable, something against which the best times are measured. But we all have our limits, the number of shots to the chops we're willing to take before the fun deteriorates into determination and, ultimately, frustration.

Larry and I gave up first and walked back to the raft, knowing that fresh red salmon are fickle fish. No one seems to know why reds, eaters of krill and plankton at sea, *ever* strike flies in freshwater. But sometimes they do, and occasionally they can be downright reckless about it.

So Larry and I sat on the raft, munching wheat crackers and gouda, watching Devon and David cast to rolling fish. About that time, a hatch of green drakes—big, juicy mayflies, a few of which had been fluttering around since late morning—suddenly seemed to intensify. Oddly enough, as the hatch progressed, so did the number of porpoising salmon. By the time Larry put down the cheese and asked if I was sure those were salmon, I was already threading floating line through the ferrules of a lighter rod.

For the next three days we watched the sky above the river, and whenever mayflies fluttered down like spring snow, we would drop our salmon rods and cast Humpys at the splashing rises. We caught many fighting Dollys, ocean-fresh, silver-sided, to three pounds. Those were rare, magical times.

———

Back on Quartz Creek, in a freshening drizzle, the pool has rested and my Dolly has returned. I've tied on a yellow #8 Marabou Muddler, deciding to beat the fish at its own game. Dollys are, above all, carnivores, notorious hunters of small fish (which is what got them that bounty rap in the first place). I've caught Dollys so full of grayling fry that they've regurgitated in the shallows as I've towed them in and in my hands as I've removed hooks from their mouths.

So now I'm standing again, peeling off line. I've got a good feeling about this. Sometimes, when you've thought a situation through and come up with the right fly, something clicks. You just *know*, before you even cast, that this time you're going to connect, just as you know before you pull the Weatherby's trigger that everything's in line and that the cackling willow ptarmigan out front is going to crumple into a stone-dead ball.

The Muddler's minuscule plunge is just another dimple among the rain drops. I've lost it against the gravel bottom. Suddenly, the Dolly is lunging forward. I haven't felt a thing, but I'm yanking back anyway, and the fish is there.

A Dolly's struggle is distinct, unmistakable. It starts off as a head-shaking, bull-dogging brawl, stubborn, extended, fading finally into a lazy, spinning reluctance. This fish is no different. There are no fancy, heart-stopping rainbow-trout leaps or sizzling runs. Just a good, solid wrestling match that makes my reel growl, my rod twitch and bow. In a few minutes I'm releasing the fish, a thick-bodied, smooth-skinned, sixteen-inch chunk. And for the moment my mystery is solved, the groundwork for the day set.

Later on, I'll catch up with David downstream. The Marabou Muddler will be the fly of the day, and we'll use them to catch a dozen or more Dollys to nearly four pounds. At one point, I run into a trio of Glo-bug-casting flyfishers working a hole. I wait and, when they leave fishless, I step in and pull out two heavy Dollys. A certain smugness will warm me in the cold drizzle; I have proven that fishing for Dollys is what you make it. Underestimate the fish, play them for fools, and the whole point of being out there is lost.

By early afternoon David and I are back in the car, wet but happy. The clouds have lifted and the rain has stopped. Sure enough, the high country now is white and I can imagine those alpine lakes, black and still against a tundra valley covered in snow. The ptarmigan are likely venturing out, feeding here and there on frost-bitten blueberries, and I'll bet the goldenfins are probably hungry as ever with the early snows portending summer's end. Last call for surface bugs. But the Dollys haven't let us down today. That's the beauty of them.

In the end, Dolly Varden are the renegades of the fishing world, once persecuted, now respected—for their beauty, for their spunk. For their ability to persevere and survive against all odds, natural and human. They are more sophisticated than we ever imagined, and as time goes on, they will likely grow more refined because Dollys are, after all, survivors. They are Alaska's fish, and with all my heart, I'm glad to have them.

Stream Maggots

Poetry found in the reflection of windless seas vanishes with the noodling frailty of light fly rods in a stiff breeze. Still, Tony Route's out there, walking on water—two, three inches deep—off a gravel spit 200 yards offshore. He's false casting into the wind, putting some shoulder into it, throwing 'em the wood. Foamy whitecaps slap his ankles; dorsals appear briefly in dancing troughs thirty, forty feet out.

"Like casting the flats for bones," Tony shouts over the surf. "Find the fish, cast in front of them."

Hunting for bonefish is a "compulsory achievement of the ever-enlarging flyfishing community," wrote author John Cole, in his book *Fish of My Years*. Truth often lurks in cynicism. But Tony stalked bones years ago, before it became fashionable. And now he's moved on—to flats as translucent and salty as those of Belize, but colder, more northerly. Now he's casting to salmon off Alaska's Gulf Coast.

We'd landed in a Cessna 185 on floats two evenings earlier on the kind of wind-whipped chop that bangs your butt and jars your kidneys loose. We'd waded up to the beach with our gear and, as the plane left us, turned our backs on the sea and set up a snug camp in some hemlocks at the mouth of a narrow creek.

The place was alive with energy; you could feel it in the pounding waves, in the sandy prints of beach-combing grizzlies. Right away, even though it was 7 P.M., we rigged fly rods, light four-weights. We hadn't eaten since breakfast. The tide was edg-

ing its way in, and fish in large schools were entering the creek—
you could see wakes and boils on the surface.

Most of us go into a fishing trip with an idea of what we will
find and how we will handle what we find, even if we've never
been there and really have no idea. A margin of error is allowed,
expected, so to compensate we come prepared for anything.
That's a good policy, particularly in Alaska, this huge, wild country that remains in many ways remote and unknown. Here,
you're always exploring.

Our agenda included anadromous fish. We expected Dolly Varden (the source, perhaps, of those incoming wakes) and, hopefully, sea-run cutthroats, known to exist in fewer than ninety
Alaskan stream systems from Ketchikan to Prince William
Sound. Salmon also were likely, silvers and pinks, but the smaller,
more exotic fish held an undeniable intrigue.

The creek's lower stretch, the flow neutralized by the incoming tide, was deep and still, and as we hiked upstream, we were
tempted by swirling fish. The water was the color of bourbon
and ice, and an overcast sky created a dull but impenetrable glare,
leaving us to guess what lay beneath. Tony and I agreed to treat
the mystery fish as Dollys, imaging them sea-fresh, bright as
dimes, marked with sea lice.

We cast various streamers and attractor patterns for an hour,
with no results. Finally, a purple Egg-sucking Leech, the ubiquitous Alaska standby, broke the ice. I'd tossed the fly into the fading rings of a swirl nearby, let it sink for a three-count, then
started stripping line. On the third strip, something heavy struck
and ran hell-bent. I shouted to Tony that I'd hooked a salmon—
a fresh silver—and for a moment I wondered if I could hold it on
a rod built for two-pound trout.

The fish didn't jump, just tore upstream like a rocket, and be-

fore I could even hope to turn it, my leader popped and the ride
was over.

Tony stood watching from the beach grass along the bank.

"Are you sure that was a silver?" he asked.

"I'd bet five bucks," I said.

There are many reasons to fish—as an excuse to explore new
places, outdoors and within ourselves, to collect experiences in
the quest of different species. And sometimes we fish to get
high—no rush compares to the blistering run of something big
tearing off with your fly, forcing you to hang on like a cowboy
busting a wild bronc. In that light, it occurred to me that the subtle attraction of the little fish—the Dollys and cutts—had suddenly vanished.

I was prepared, minutes later, with heavier leader and lighter
drag when the next salmon struck. The strike was vicious, literally
stinging my palm, the run fast, like the first. Another silver. This
time I hung on until the fish turned and shot straight past me, allowing me to gain line, reeling furiously. The struggle lasted perhaps ten minutes, and when it was over, I reached into the brackish water and, to my shock, pulled out a pink salmon.

A humpy. A stream maggot. Due to its commonness and
grotesque hunch-backed appearance on spawning beds, probably the most disrespected gamefish in Alaska.

Tony stood on the bank and laughed—belly-laughed—for a
long time.

So now Tony's out on the flats, casting white streamers that resemble squid to packs of hunting dorsals. I'm watching, curious,
still smarting a bit from that first night, more open-minded now,
ready to learn. Tony's line suddenly snaps tight, and he's leaning

into his six-weight rod—a stick that is a little heavier, but not *too* heavy (the right rod, he tells me, is the secret to appreciating any fish). The struggle is brutal, faster than the gusting wind. Tan fly line rips across the troughs, leaving traces of foam bobbing on top.

I'm still thinking about that first night, how I'd entered a new dimension in sport, one that I'd found addictive, that kept me out way too late, even though fried sausage and a shot of good Scotch waited in a lonely camp a half mile away. That, of course, is what it's all about—the searching, discovering, the rush along the way.

Tony's kneeling in the salty shallows, freeing another pink salmon. I'll never again see them the same way. Before I realize it, I'm wading out there again myself.

Fall

North Fork

Every so often, when I stop and look back on my life, I can see that it has been punctuated by periods of craziness where I have forgotten my head and followed my heart. I am an impulsive creature. Something within is pulled and tweaked like the tides by the moon, loose screws rattle, biorhythms idle out of control. It's a cyclical thing for me, aligned perfectly with seasons in transition—fall particularly.

Here's the deal. On a given day in September, on high plains of dwarf birch (thigh-high shrubs with round, dime-like leaves the color of fire), I might find myself gripping a walnut-stocked .30-06 as caribou trot by in migrating bands; or perhaps I will be casting a #14 Black Gnat over rising grayling in tannic tundra streams. At the same time, spruce grouse cluck in boreal cranberry patches, and on dry afternoons I might end up following a yellow, square-headed bitch through musky alder tangles, double-gun in hand, heart fibrillating in anticipation of the flush.

Too, silver salmon are running—swarming, writhing schools of them—and the rainbow lakes have come alive. Simply put, fall is an exasperating time where everything in my life that is good merges at once, pressing me to define myself and choose between my passions. It's like choosing between my daughters—I will not do it—and in the end I'm caught trying to do everything at once. This is the madness of fall.

Summer now is fading. The first signs have appeared in the stream bottom and in the muskegs where early frosts settle. Willows and cottonwoods blaze along the bars in vivid yellow and copper tones; rose hips hang from hairy-legged stalks, shriveled, like scarlet, seedy prunes. The air, muggy back in June and July, now is cool, fragrant with the slightly sweet, slightly sour smell of ripe highbush cranberries.

Spawned-out salmon, chums and pinks, are strewn helter-skelter along the creek bank, forming a battle scene of grimacing bodies. I'll try to step around them as I make my way upstream, less out of respect than because they're slippery under felt-bottomed wading soles. The stench of decaying fish seems at first overpowering, but after a while, you get used to it. It's part of the chain of life: the carcasses dissolve into the stream, ultimately providing a legacy of proteins and other nutrients vital to newly-hatched progeny.

I'm getting away now, from the road, from a part of myself held prisoner by work, relationships, the necessary evils of society. Got to keep on walking.

Mud. Gravel. Brush. Bear tracks. A pebble-picking covey flushes underfoot, sends my heart into spasms, the big rifle off my shoulder. An hour has passed. I'm standing at the tail end of a pool, watching a knot of silver salmon holding against the far bank. I've come expecting smaller fish—three-pound rainbow trout, perhaps a grayling or two. My four-weight seems suddenly puny. Still, I kneel to lower my profile and pull a fly box from my vest.

How many times have I lived this moment, dreamed it, savored it? Enough to know about the violence and spite that silvers embody, the piss and gall that makes them supreme gamefish. Enough to know that fall comes but once a year and, this far north, passes too quickly. Every cool, drizzling, champagne minute is precious and begs to be tasted. Winter will come one windless night, like the echo of an iron gate closing. Here to stay.

The silvers. They despise the old Alaskan standby, the Egg-sucking Leech. Sends them into furies. A #4 should do it.

Third drift: a ribald buck bolts out of formation and grabs my fly, twisting, gnashing like a ten-pound shark. He's testing my tackle, running downstream until I put on more pressure, then thrashing madly on top, threatening to pop the light tippet.

The following minutes are important; I play give-and-take, keeping just enough tension on the line, allowing the salmon to wear itself out. It tires within five minutes or so (sooner than you might expect, unless you take into account how far it has traveled, blindly up the silty Susitna to this tributary flowing out of the Talkeetna Mountains), allowing me to lead it ashore, head shaking in weakening spasms. The coup de grâce is sudden, brutal: a whack with a rock between those hawkish salmon eyes.

This is fall—the tickling current, the fragrant berries, the cold blood leaving those silver gills and painting my fingers red. It all will end next week, with the Weber grill and a rack of glowing coals, fillets glistening in a marinade of soy sauce, brown sugar, ground ginger, pressed garlic, and orange juice. Slap 'em on the grill, skin-side down, sizzling, till the scales char. Serve with baked potatoes and ice-cold beer.

Within twenty minutes I've whacked two more. Others remain, so I continue casting, breaking off a couple, and landing and releasing a few more. After that, the fishing slows and I take a moment to squat by the stream and gut my catch. I'll tuck them in the willows on a mat of brown grass where they will stay wet and fresh until I pick them up later. I need to find some rainbows.

This little creek (two guys holding nine-foot rods on opposite banks could almost touch tips in the narrower sections) came as a surprise. It's fished murderously for kings in the spring and early summer and gets almost as much attention in August when the first silvers run, and for years I'd written it off. Too much pressure. But things change up here in September—particularly on the small streams—when there are moose, Dall sheep, caribou, and ducks to hunt. The salmon-crazies have their freezers filled. It's time to pack what space is left with red meat.

But one gloomy Sunday too wet for moose hunting, I drove on up to kill some time and savor the air. No one else was there and I found plenty of silvers, trout, and grayling. Ever since, this stream, on this date, has had its special place in my bag of tricks. I call it North Fork.

A few turns up from the silver hole, I break through an alder thicket and step onto an open bar. Beyond the gravel, a deep, gentle bend flanked on each end by riffles, promises trout. So I slip down to the shoreline and, within a couple of casts, I'm into— surprise!—another silver salmon. Over the next half hour, I end up landing and releasing several bright salmon until finally, casting to a small white flash, I sense a pluck. I set the hook and can tell by the soft, flitting struggle that I've hooked a grayling.

How those small, pouting mouths engulf the bends of #4 streamer hooks I do not know. But they do so often. The grayling prances delicately in the riffles, briefly, then raises its broad fin and surrenders on one side, eyes crossing, gaping at the hook. The fish is pot-bellied from choking down salmon eggs. I grab the grayling just behind its pectorals, slip the hook from its mouth and let go, watching. It gropes in the shallows for a moment, perplexed, then darts into the deep, dark water.

The air this time of year is filled with a sense of desperation. Another summer is slipping through my fingers, like one last, good fish. The feeling is like waking up one morning to discover half your life has passed by, the good times too quickly gone. Where, in fact, did the summer go? How did another one pass by without a sound, and where, in the scheme of things, does this leave me? So, in fall, I seek footholds among ferns withered by frost, casting with an intensity that is manic, unrivaled.

A couple of bends up, I'm shuffling alongside a set of riffles that gallop among stones that form deep, calm pockets. My fly falls behind a moss-topped boulder and, before I'm ready, I feel a spiteful yank. There's no mistaking the strike of a rainbow, especially when it grabs your fly and burns off thirty feet of line before you can react.

This fish is heavy, forceful, and runs straight downstream, making me splash through the shallows in pursuit. Rainbows are my favorites, the way they leap and run with a power and stamina as pure and reckless as life itself. By the time I catch up, the trout has had a moment to rest in an eddy beneath some overhanging alders on the creek's far side. Still, I'm gaining, putting on some pressure. Sometimes you've got to dog these fish, keep them moving and tire them out.

I'm too late. The trout has found its second wind and is now tearing upstream. I'm stumbling over cobbles, cussing softly. The fish jumps, tumbles over the stream, gives me a good view—I guess it'll go four or five pounds.

There are more trying moments, as my leader wraps around a rock when the trout dashes upstream then darts suddenly back down. Somehow, by lifting my rod high above my head, I manage to free the mess before the fish can break off. Signs of tiring—false surrenders into the shallows followed by shorter, less determined runs—come gradually. But eventually, grudgingly, the trout gives in.

Evening kind of creeps up on you this time of year, sort of like winter. One minute you look up from what you're doing and it's just there. I've been at it all afternoon and am playing another rainbow—a leaping, shaking, pink-sided sprite—when a loon in flight calls overhead. The overcast skies have grown dark, heavy. Rain is starting to fall in icy, silver drops.

I'll play this last one out, then reel up and walk downstream to that cache of salmon. We'll have one hell of a barbecue when the rain lets up. Of course, it may not stop until October. And then it will turn to snow.

River of
Questions

I am kneeling on the verge of a remote Southwest river, searching for answers in fluttering reflections of tundra and sky. In
one hand, I'm gripping a nine-foot fly rod, in the other a hank of
tinsel and deer hair, clipped and dyed an unlikely hot-pink. Spun
on a hook that is sharp and silver, it is a gaudy affair: part Vegas,
part L.L. Bean. Called a Pink Pollywog by the few who use it,
the fly floats—unlike most Pacific salmon flies—like a cork.

Bulling upstream in gangs, fixed on destinations etched deeply
within genetic maps, silver salmon flood the river in a living
surge. They arrive here this time each year, in the waning days of
summer when the air grows damp and cold, and the blueberries,
past prime, go mushy and saccharin.

This is *extreme* fishing, because there are so many salmon and
because the only way to experience it—other than by running a
riverboat a hundred miles upstream from a coastal Eskimo village—is to ride the current, as I have, on a raft from the river's
source at a great tundra lake. The rewards are solitude and, if you
care to drift a Battle Creek Special or a pink Babine Special, a
salmon on nearly every cast.

In fact, I've worn out my forearm using streamers to catch fish
after fish, and the excitement that came with the first few battles
has faded, grown decidedly banal. At its best, fishing is a river of

questions not yet asked and answers that remain to be revealed. When things get too predictable, it is time to move on. So here I am, trying to convince fasting fish to turn 180 degrees against their nature to bite a dry fly dressed like a flamboyant whore.

In Alaskan streams dry-fly fishing is usually reserved for smaller fish, typically grayling. Sail-finned bug-eaters with dainty, pouting mouths, grayling are renowned surface-feeders. Dry flies such as Black Gnats, Humpys or Renegades, nearly anything resembling a floating lunch, will interest them. As a kid, I once tossed a wood frog the size of a quarter into an old dredge pond boiling with rising grayling. The frog kicked once, twice, then disappeared in a swirling rise.

Of course, ocean-fresh silver salmon are not dainty bug-eaters (though I wonder if a frog thrown in at the right place, at the right time ...). Still, they are known for belligerent streaks that send them out of their way to strike cured spawn or stripped streamers—the result, perhaps, of territorial impulses or not-yet-forgotten feeding reflexes.

I encountered an example of this belligerence years ago while fishing bait for silvers in a Susitna River tributary. Frustrated at snagging the weedy bottom, I clipped a red bobber above my hook. The bobber allowed my bait to float above the weeds, and I caught a limit of bright silvers almost as fast as I could reel them in. But I also noticed something odd. For every fish I hooked, another would charge the surface like a hungry shark to grab my bobber.

This aggressive spark, this willingness to rise to meet a challenge, is what defines silver salmon as popular sport fish. It also makes catching them on dry flies a distinct possibility.

Treeless hills roll away from the river, appearing as swells on a tundra sea. A squall is settling in, for an hour, a day, a week; the sky in this part of Alaska, always moody, becomes schizophrenic in fall. A breeze that has cooled my cheeks all day suddenly dies, as sometimes happens in the moments preceding a passionate rain.

In front of me, off the main current, a slough is the perfect stage for my experiment; a cluster of undulating shadows is gathered a short cast away. Determined as they are to reach sacred gravel, silvers are notorious dawdlers, hopelessly drawn to frog-water—languid creek mouths, stagnant backwaters—where they loiter like truant punks in dark arcades.

Fearing that a fly dropped directly on top of the fish might cause them to spook, I cast several feet ahead of them. The silvers wince visibly when my Pink Pollywog plops onto the surface, and for a moment, the world freezes.

It is easy at times like this to wonder if I've made the right choice; something more traditional like an Egg-sucking Leech or a green-and-white tarpon fly would have been a sure bet. But there is a point where simply *catching* fish becomes redundant. And in the end, you recognize that "sport" and "challenge" are relative terms and sometimes you need to do whatever it takes to simply have a good time.

The salmon appear nervous, treading just off the bottom, shaking their heads faintly. Impulsively, I twitch my rod tip and the Pollywog struts sharply toward me, leaving a tiny wake. The salmon grow still; I have their attention.

Another twitch and the entire group of salmon—six or eight of them—gravitate toward the fly. Now I'm twitching my rod in short, continuous pecks, causing the fly to break the surface in tiny splashes. That's all it takes. A heavy buck with a faint ruddy blush bolts so fast that I have no time to react. It is as if tension in a hard-steel spring were suddenly released. There is a violent explosion of water, then a familiar surging tautness as my fly line cuts across the slough.

The salmon leaps again and again, my pink dry fly a visible contradiction in the corner of its mouth. Suddenly, in the rush of the battle, I become conscious of myself: I am a shouting, tiny speck in the center of a tundra-and-water universe. For the moment, my question is lost to the answer; there is nothing in the world except for me and a salmon dancing where the water meets the sky.

Three Rivers

Time has its own agenda, there's no stopping it.
—Maurice Minniefield,
Northern Exposure

So, in the scheme of the land, a vacuum of tundra, water, rock and space, it is easy to become lost. Here, where the human spirit withers in the presence of unclimbed mountains and anonymous streams, you may see yourself for what you really are: a throbbing mote, a tiny composite of dimly charged matter. This is subarctic Alaska, a place where perspective is born.

We are flying over a soggy muskeg plain west of Dillingham. Mountains erupt suddenly through moody veils of wind-driven rain. Pilot Lester Bingman, thirtyish, heavyset, with the blunt, unpolished face of a Skid Row bouncer, is fabled for his familiarity with the Wood River Mountains.

"I fly low," he says. "I know all the trails." Bravado in the tenor of young aviators evokes concern (*There are old pilots and bold pilots, but …*); for an instant my stomach twists.

Bingman's trails, it turns out, are rivers—the Wood, the Snake, the Weary—pouring from long, narrow mountain lakes fifteen, twenty roadless miles beyond Dillingham. The lakes taper into canyons, gnawed by retreating glaciers, twisting among broken crags, and forming on topographic maps and in the brains of savvy pilots a great vermicular labyrinth. On days like this, when the land smolders in cold mist and the skies sulk under ugly

Bering Sea fronts, the canyons often are blocked by pea-soup fogs. Mangled bits of colored aluminum scattered across scree slopes mark the end of pilots who realized too late that there is no room for U-turns.

But Bingman, I discover, is by nature and necessity a damn good pilot. On an average day between May and late September, he spends more hours in the cockpit than on the ground. He seems connected to his plane, an integral organ, vital, natural. And he knows his way around the maze.

Under a low ceiling that buries two-thousand-foot peaks, we weave among canyon walls, hugging the contours close enough to see things: rock slides, bear trails, individual willow shrubs. On the lip of a plunging saddle, a lone caribou bull shakes its rack in a halo of blood-sucking flies. Uninitiated equilibriums spin, stomachs churn, the situation nearly desperate, when the range opens suddenly into a steel-gray lake tossing nervously in the wind. Simultaneously awestruck, mortified, and holding back a belly full of motion sickness, the first phase of a seven-day passage is complete. Another float trip begins.

The river is a silver vein, conveyor of water and things that float. It is a highway for men and for swimming creatures, a metronome which measures time. This is the Goodnews, conceived of snowmelt siphoned through tannic heath and collected in a maternal lake, a great, mountain-flanked wonder.

My friends are puttering on the beach, stringing fly rods, fitting leaders, digging into blue, red, and yellow rubber canoe bags. A raft rests inflated at the water's edge, ready for passage downriver. The atmosphere trembles with a collective eagerness to get on with it, to fish, to smell the fragrance of willow smudges on buggy, fishy evenings. The river, thankfully, is patient.

I'm walking the shoreline to the outlet where the Goodnews pours through a fold in a tundra valley. I've got my six-weight and a vest full of flies. David, Larry, and Gene will catch up.

We arrived an hour earlier aboard Bingman's Grumman Goose, an amphibious, twin-engined seaplane that lands in lakes and oceans on its boat-like belly. We were disgorged immediately, along with our gear, and as we fumbled in a fog of mild displacement, the plane roared mightily and vanished into a high valley at the lake's far end. Now the land hums with an energy that is natural, a combination of wind and river flowing against objects that resist motion, and glows with an aura that is awesome, ageless, surreal, severe. We're adapting by the minute, preparing for our roles in a continuum that will include the river, the raft, and ourselves.

The Goodnews wanders from the mountains modestly at first, gathering, as it flows, a fullness that is sleek and direct. The river delivers to the land a bounty of fish—salmon mostly (kings, sockeyes, pinks, chums, and silvers) and rainbow trout, grayling, and Dolly Varden. The salmon stage each summer in Goodnews Bay, a connection sixty river miles—seven day's float—downstream.

Now, in August's final days, the channel is a vermilion ribbon of gravid sockeyes—red salmon—mixed with a few humpbacked pinks and the odd hook-nosed silver. I'm kneeling at the river's edge, tentative, eyes on green shadows hovering behind vacillating reds. Dollys.

Time passes, a few minutes, an hour. Voices, incongruent, ghostly, slide downriver toward me. I'm releasing another Dolly, a two-pounder, pink-spotted, red-bellied, that fell for a Battle Creek Special, an orange streamer that mimics clustered salmon eggs or a ragged chunk of flesh. My friends have appeared from nowhere, perched on the raft, eager to cast and to travel. Ahead, a progression awaits—of water, fish, country, and life.

Late August in southwestern Alaska is a time of transition: Advancing nights push the days aside; tundra swans and green-winged teal fly down the river, confused, frantic. Mornings dawn damp and gray over gravel bar campsites; the air is bone-cold and raw. Noses drip, eyes water. Before camp is broken, the wind freshens and mountains surrounding the river dissolve in gathering fog. The raft and the river, vehicle and impetus, wait.

By evening you'll be in another country, where willows grow taller and the mountains stand farther away. Squalls settle in, the wind howls, and low clouds swirl around neoprene-clad knees. Yet in between outbursts of wind and drizzle, incredible breaks occur, where the air calms suddenly and the sun appears briefly to glint off eight-weight rods and porpoising dorsals.

Day three, midday. We've rounded a bend in the wind's lee; David has spotted the backs of silver salmon breaking water in the stillness of a beaver slough. Gene, the consummate flyfisher, reaches for his heavy rod; Larry leans into the oars, crosscurrent, getting us there. On float trips, you learn to steal opportunities like this, realizing that your time on the river is finite, dictated by the current's speed, a sum of gradient and gravity.

The raft has hardly landed in a mire of boot-sucking swamp and grass armpit-high when we all jump ship with our long graphite rods. Streamers, sailing for salmon marked by swirls and rolling backs, whistle past ears tucked under warm wool caps. David sticks the first fish, a crazy, leaping silver hen. I reel up, watching, waiting, and when finally it is time, grab the spent fish by its tail and hoist it ashore.

As we've drifted downriver, the spawning red salmon and pinks have all but disappeared, giving way to silver salmon that at first are black-faced, scarlet-sided. Now, thirty miles closer to Goodnews Bay, the silvers have grown abundant, fresh. Call it a movable feast, a living progression.

For the next three days, each opportunity to fish is seized and savored, then it's back in the raft, riding the river, the carrier, perpetual motion defined. The passing of time here is manifest—that is a float trip's main annoyance. The river is a clock, the current a measure of present, past, and future.

Evenings in camp are cherished things. On the river you are a nomad, moving always, putting days and miles behind you. A destination in time and place waits ahead, where the trip will be over and you will return to civilization and a life temporarily forgotten. But camp, at the day's end, offers a moment of pause where you can absorb your surroundings, take as long as you want to really work a gorgeous run.

Everyone else has gone to bed, someone is snoring in the tent shared by Gene and Larry. I'm fishing some riffles in front of camp, in the dusk, beneath the silent wings of passing ducks. I'm sticking fat Dollys with almost every cast, savoring each fish and every solitary moment. My heart beats gently, following the rhythm of the river. The sense of peace is unrivaled.

Tomorrow we will reach saltwater. A middle-aged Eskimo named James Bright will arrive by riverboat at a designated point near the river's mouth to ferry us across the bay to Goodnews Village. We will deflate the raft and throw everything into the boat. Then James, wearing Raybans and smoking a Winston, will turn his ball cap backwards, ignite the outboard, and have us up on step in the wakes of diving mergansers. At that moment, our lives will accelerate; a franticness, displaced by a week on the river, will return. *Home, James.* Doesn't sound like good news at all.

Such is the way of rivers. They take you for a ride, but eventually you must step off. Some rivers are long, others are not. In the end, it is where a river takes you—what you find along the way—that matters.

The upper Kenai is a short stretch of river, a twelve-mile connection between two great lakes, Kenai and Skilak, known as the Upper Dozen. Its color is distinctive, a glacial green that is gemlike, translucent to varying degrees, depending upon the season. On hot July days, as distant glaciers melt, the river swells, growing nearly opaque, like pea soup. But in January, free of silty runoff, the Kenai's color is more like an old fruit jar, off-green, but generally clear.

Now it is mid-September and the river is low. A score of frosty dawns has torched gravel bar willows and hills of second-growth birch; the contrast is surreal: picture an emerald ribbon parting a tart, yellow valley. I'm standing at the head of a narrow channel with Walt, my father-in-law, who is up from British Columbia to visit his first granddaughter and to fish a little. My friend Paul is pulling an inflatable raft out of the current—two rubber pontoons connected by an aluminum frame sprouting three swivel seats—and our knuckles are red and raw from a cold morning rain that let up minutes ago, leaving the valley wet and the mountain tops white.

The upper Kenai's main stem is swift, broad, and intimidating. It is like Alaska in general, too big to take on all at once and therefore best fished in pieces. So when we can, we work the channels—narrow, creek-like meanderings, readable microcosms with discernible pools and runs.

The first channel we come to is one that I've fished many times before. It wanders for a half mile or so between an alder flat and a high, sprucy bank and, depending upon the fishing, takes an hour or two to properly explore. Red salmon, spawned-out, tattered caricatures with hooked kypes and worried eyes, wait to die in the pools. The shallows are littered with moldy carcasses of others whose sacrifice is complete. In the dark water, beneath cutbanks and overhanging alders, trout—some weighing twenty pounds—wait like wolves for stray salmon eggs and pieces of drifting flesh.

I can trace the first rainbow trout of my life to the upper Kenai River. I was a crew-cut five-year-old, chubby with pink cheeks, strapped in a flare-orange life vest. The air, as usual, was cool and wet, and I held a short fiberglass rod, white with red wrap. My reel was a cheap single action, spray-painted red, and I sat on a bank, soaking salmon roe with strict instructions not to move. Mid-river, across a channel not likely as wide as I remember, my father and a friend cast streamers over a bottomless run. No boats on the river then, the mid-1960s, and not another angler in sight.

My line tightened suddenly as I sat there; it made me curious. I lifted the rod and something tugged. I wanted to stand, but knew I must not, so I held on, and when a splashing fish fluttered across my eddy, I began to shout. From there the memory fades, but I landed that trout and one other before the day's end. A long-lost photograph records it all: pot-bellied child gripping two white-eyed, scarlet-sided Kenai River rainbows, lovely three-pound fish twisted in full-blown rigor mortis.

This morning the Upper Dozen is a freeway for driftboats with up-turned prows, dozens of them, manned by fly-vested oarsmen and rod-holding passengers. All of them sport "special" fishing hats they believe to be distinct; they're trying to separate themselves from the rest of the crowd, but they all look the same to me.

Fortunately, we have the channels, miles of them winding off from the main river, allowing space and isolation and fine small-stream flycasting. I'm pitching a home-tied Marabou Muddler into some riffles below a pool filled with terminal red salmon. Among the alders, lime-green stoneflies are hatching, tiny things no larger than mosquitoes. A trout, looks like a small one, is feeding on flickering stoneflies at the tail of the pool. I dropped my Muddler on him five minutes ago and put him down, but now he's back. Walt has worked downstream a ways and Paul is above me, tying on a fly.

Visitors are impressed by Alaska and Alaskans love to impress visitors. For three hours, as we drove in the dark to the rhythm of beating windshield wipers, I told Walt about the Kenai River. I mentioned the river's famous rainbow trout, the twenty-pounders, and the ubiquitous Dolly Varden, reaching twelve pounds. I told him the story about being spooled by the big rainbow where the Russian River meets the Kenai and how I'd been forced to grip the last of my line and break the fish off because I didn't trust my twelve-pound backing. But Walt is a gentle man not easily taken by hyperbole.

My Muddler bounces down the riffles, past the scarlet shadows of hovering red salmon. Then, dead ahead, an olive-topped, pink-sided hulk appears. *Ambush!* The take is instantaneous, and I reef back on my eight-weight. The fish is long and it runs straight downstream, black-flecked back tearing through the riffles.

In a flash, I'm hollering. "Walt! It's one of the big ones. Rainbow!" I am insane, shouting, stumbling over the cobbles, screwing with my drag.

Walt reels up, watches me over one shoulder as the fish peels line and plunges into the pool at his feet. I'm getting things under control. There in the pool, the fish feels more secure; it doesn't leap, just runs deep, bulldogging, head shaking. Upstream, Paul is casting to the little stonefly-sipping trout, looking my way now and then, monitoring the situation with the casualness of a man who has seen his share of large fish caught.

The struggle goes nowhere fast. For a long time, it's just me standing near the water gripping a throbbing stick. Walt starts to wander downstream, but I stop him, tell him he must see this.

Finally, I've worked the fish into the shallows. It is lovely, perhaps twelve, fourteen pounds. I can hear gravel crunching under
Walt's boots as he steps alongside. There's something strange
about this trout. The pink stripe seems too broad, lacks a certain
definition. And then my cheeks flush, grow hot. *Never mind,
Walt. It's a silver salmon.*

The upper Kenai has changed with Alaska. As the population has
grown—we are now the *third* least populated state—so has the
fishing pressure. Since it is glacial, the river once went largely
overlooked by all but a sneaky, meat-fishing few who slipped off
the Sterling Highway in July to snag red salmon. Then came the
flyfishing boom of the late 1980s and word got around that the
Upper Dozen wasn't half bad for trout and Dollys; in fact, in
September, it was damn good. Cooper Landing, through which
the upper Kenai runs, became a village of fishing guides. Now
the river has become a sort of world-famous institution. And so
the familiar progression goes.

Recently, the upper Kenai has become a small-scale Yellowstone, a place where civilization and wilderness merge and min-
gle. Earlier in the summer, I'd drifted the Upper Dozen with my
wife and Greg-the-Cop. The reds had just arrived, fresh-minted,
silver-sided thousands of them, and the usual salmon-hungry
crowds swarmed the Russian River confluence where we put in.
But soon we were drifting, and within ten minutes, things began
to settle down. We had just rounded the first bend when we spotted a young grizzly, a two year old, on the bank. The creature
stood still, watching us with tiny, wild eyes, pink tongue lolling
like a big dog. We passed silently within forty or fifty feet of the
bear, watched it turn without alarm into the trees. Sonnie was impressed, having never seen a grizzly so close.

A quarter mile downstream, we beached the raft on a gravel bar and started casting. I'd picked up a ten-inch rainbow and Greg was into a Dolly when Sonnie shouted. I turned around and saw the small grizzly waddling in pigeon-toed bear fashion down the bar toward our raft. A couple of anglers between us and the bear rushed out of the current and ran downstream. One of them yelled that the young bear's mother was coming, too. Sonnie, Greg, and I walked up to the raft and pulled it into the current. The small grizzly stopped, watched myopically, and again headed for the brush. In a moment, we were swept away. Never did see the sow.

Weeks later, the newspapers reported a young grizzly was shot and killed on the upper Kenai. No one seemed to know why. That may be the main difference between the Kenai and the Yellowstone: the tourists here are packing heat.

But now it is September, and Walt, Paul, and I are back on the Kenai's swift main stem. We've seen no bears and little sign, but we did end up catching several rainbows in that narrow channel. Nothing over three pounds.

Bald eagles, "fish buzzards," perch in tall cottonwoods on each side of the river. Boats are everywhere, upstream, downstream, pulled up on bars. At one point, we pass a guide I once hired to take me and some friends fishing. He stares with icy, territorial eyes as we pass. For a moment, I feel like a trespasser; then I remember the photograph—that crew-cut kid, those first rainbow trout. The river does the rest, carries us off, out of sight.

Rivers flow and wander and stretch out, even short sections like the Kenai's Upper Dozen. Popular as the river is, you need not look far to find fishy, unpeopled bars. By late afternoon, the sun has broken through and the cobbles have dried. Paul, normally cheerful, has had trouble connecting and has grown intense, focused. I've just broken my leader on an old red buck and am tying on a new fly. That's when I hear Paul's drag buzzing.

After you've caught a few of your own, there is nothing more satisfying than watching a friend tie into a nice fish. In a way, it's sort of like having an out-of-body experience; you can put yourself in his place and enjoy the rapture from angles otherwise impossible to see. I drop everything and walk up to watch. Paul is leaning into the fish, smiling broadly, the way he does after work when he's sitting down with a cold beer. The struggle is short, a heavy, throbbing urgency that never breaks the surface. Then he reaches into the shallows and pulls out a lovely four-pound Dolly Varden.

Walt is gone, having worked somewhere down around the bend, so I pick up my rod and start walking that way. A few minutes later, I can see him fishing a seam where the river slips past a pool of dead water. Back in July, when we had seen the bear, I'd watched my wife—Walt's daughter—catch her first fresh red salmon in the same seam. Before I can say anything, Walt's drift stops abruptly, his rod lurches forward. The fish rushes upstream madly, leaps a couple of times, then turns and heads for the pool. Rainbow.

Again, I'm pleased to be watching, enjoying the fact that, in a multi-generational sort of way, things seem to be coming around full circle. One day, perhaps, I will fish this river with my young daughters and the circle will grow larger.

Walt takes his time, savors the synergy of struggling trout and hissing current. But all rides must end eventually and the fish swaggers finally into the dead water. The rainbow is not particularly long, barely twenty inches, but it is deep-bodied, obese. I mention that this is Sonnie's pool and Walt smiles, says nothing, just watches his fish splash desperately back into the river.

We work a few more channels after that, short, narrow, grassy ones, picking up a few more trout and Dollys. Then the sun ducks behind the Kenai Mountains, and the air becomes cold, edgy, promising frost. One moment we're drifting a secluded channel, the next we're back out on the main river in sight of tents and campers and great mobs of boats. Jim's Landing. This is where we get off. It's been ten hours, yet I can't help feeling like we've only gotten started. We're hungry and probably more tired than we know. But if there was time, I would propose packing up, driving back to the top, and starting all over.

Rivers are that way: they deliver us, provide for our starving souls. You need only hop aboard and let the current take you along. Some journeys are longer than others, yet when you reach the end, you look back and realize that life is indeed a river, and the river is always too short.

⸺⁓⸺

The Gulkana seems subdued. Or perhaps it's only me. In years past I've watched her amber waters sparkle, heard her riffles sing. But I've been gone awhile. And now, in late August, the river shuffles soberly along, muttering over rocks, oddly preoccupied.

The big sleep's coming. You can feel it in the freezer-locker bite of the morning air, smell it in the cabernet fragrance of berries fermenting, see it in the explosions of color all around— blood-reds, yellows, oranges like flame. The world is changing; somehow the river seems to know.

I'm standing knee-deep in the Gulkana's west fork, a remote, unpeopled vein, my five-weight tucked under one arm, tying on a Black Gnat. The pool is deep, maybe twelve feet, and a good, long double-haul across. A grayling breaks the surface upriver, out of range. Another boils a rod's length from my waders. Too close. Then I hear a faint slap, perhaps thirty feet out and slightly downstream. One more falsecast and there …

The fish is up in an instant, sucking down the fly, and then with a splash, it is dashing for the bottom. I yank up my rod tip, feeling the resistance. The fish surges, leaps, and we struggle for several minutes, each giving and taking line by the cold, dripping yard.

Finally, the grayling turns on its side and I'm kneeling in the shallows, reaching. Now the river is a mirror framing a world of blazing willows, black spruce barrens, and rolling tundra hills. It all seems so familiar. In the center of it all hovers the reflection of a boy wearing a fly vest and an expression of recognition. I'm wondering, *Have we met?* Then I'm dipping into the looking glass, pulling out the blue-and-purple fish, and the river's spell is abruptly broken.

There is something about this Interior country—specifically, the Copper River Basin—that draws me unlike any other place. It is a land of anonymous lakes and of rivers with musical titles, like Nelchina, Oshetna, Tyone, Gulkana. The land and its waters are unique in a sense that is singularly Alaskan, set apart not only by name, but in context, texture, and mood.

More, perhaps, than anything else, this country and I share a common past:

I'm six-years-old, casting a second-hand bamboo fly rod over a narrow Nelchina River tributary, already a veteran of the August hunts that will bring me here with my family for many years to come. Grayling are leaping for mosquitoes when, on the far bank, a caribou bull appears, looming, larger than life. Thirty years later I can still look into these waters and see, amid the feeding grayling and those far-away tundra hills, that animal's face. Deer and fish. They're icons of this wild place and no matter where life takes me or how long I'm away, the three of us will remain connected.

I'm here today on the Gulkana's west fork with Larry Hagen, who pilots the raft, and his longtime friend, Gene Lorenson, of Spokane. Gene is a driven, contemporary rendition of the compleat angler who is along for the ride, casting his way through nirvana.

We'd stepped into the country two nights earlier, an hour before the stars came out, delivered by a Beaver, a stubby, pontooned bush plane. Our pilot, a bass-throated Lee Marvin replica named Bart, put us down on Fish Lake (one of at least sixteen Fish Lakes in Alaska, suggesting a profusion of fertile Alaskan lakes, or a paucity of imagination on the part of Alaskans). Caribou bands pranced along the lake shore, and when Bart cut the throttle and we opened the plane's riveted metal doors, you could hear caribou all around the lake snorting and grunting, busting brush.

We set up camp on the beach and inflated our raft, preparing for the three-day float that would take us down Fish Lake, through a mile-long outlet stream to the Gulkana and downriver to Sourdough on the Richardson Highway. The lake was flat as a table top and whitefish wallowed and swirled along its edges. For thirty minutes, as dusk rose like inky smoke from the taiga, Gene and I stood on the gravel shoreline casting. The fish were strong, deep-bodied, bronze-sided, and if three-pound whitefish can't jump, they certainly can sprint and cut the surface sprightly with their muscular humped backs.

Now it is dawn on the river and the autumn sun is distant and cold. Larry's stirring up blueberry pancakes in a plastic bowl, and Gene is standing below me catching big Gulkana River grayling.

That first day, as we prepared to row down Fish Lake in Larry's raft, I'd left camp on foot with my rifle over one shoulder. Caribou cows and calves grazed along the lake shore, grunting and bouncing through the willows. At one point, I'd stalked a huge, white-maned bull. I might have got him, but he'd been with his harem and there had been too many eyes. Some vigilant cow caught me moving, and the entire herd had vanished in a bug-eyed stampede of splayed hooves and flashing white rumps.

I'd caught up with Larry and Gene later that morning. We floated down the meandering outlet stream and reached the west fork around lunch time. We were pulled up on a gravel bar, munching pilot bread and cheese, when three caribou bulls appeared upriver on the opposite bank. I'd picked up my rifle, aimed slightly over a medium bull's neck, and squeezed. We'd dressed the caribou in a light drizzle, swatting at whitesocks, the tiny bloodsucking gnats of fall.

So, this morning, Gene and I are working that long, deep pool, catching the chunky grayling. I'm listening to the hustling river, thinking about yesterday's blood, the grisliness of it, and the necessity, happy now just fishing.

"Kid," wrote William Kittredge in *Owning it All*, "she's a new world every morning." And she is. Particularly when you're floating a river. (Hell, she's a new world every *minute* then.)

Yet in a broad sense, the world here appears unchanged, despite my absence and the unstoppable passage of years. The hills, the water, the fish and game, the cool grayness of morning in late August—these things remain as I remember them. Wild. Pure. And something about that satisfies me deeply.

Just Before
Winter

Even as it draws me, I am frightened by September in a way that is in one sense overwhelming and, in another, sensual. The season now is in transition, and time doesn't linger the way it does in January's post-solstice darkness or during July's endless days. Life, for the moment, accelerates, the days measured as grains in an hourglass, appearing to fall ever faster near autumn's end.

I'm standing on the shore of a nameless lake in the snow-covered taiga of the Nelchina Basin, watching a band of caribou—a dozen or so, all cows and calves—hustle through stubby black spruce on the lake's far side. In spite of the snow, the lake remains ice-free, though sullen and dark in contrast. I left a fly rod back at camp and, in my heart, am dying to find out what secrets the lake might hold. But there is hunting to do, and until I kill a caribou, fishing must wait.

I watch the cows and calves until they are out of sight, then sit down to wait for more animals to pass. I'll take a barren cow if I must, but a bull would be better—more meat for my effort.

Caribou are funny animals, bug-eyed, neurotic, nomadic. Always in a hurry, they are will-o'-the-wisps, sweeping the Nelchina country in great herds one day, gone for Canada the next. I've hunted them for three decades, yet they remain no more predictable than the weather. Familiar, perhaps, but not predictable.

We'd flown in the evening before with Charlie Akers, a Lake Louise bush pilot who looks a lot like Dustin Hoffman but with round, wire-rimmed glasses and a Pepperidge Farms accent. Akers suggested, as Larry and I loaded our gear into the float-plane, that we alter our strategy and hunt farther north than we'd planned. The caribou had moved beyond the hills of nearby Grayling Lake, he said. Three days earlier, the area had crawled with them. Now they were gone.

Of course, Akers added, the extra flight time would cost us each fifty bucks extra. Larry winced, but Akers gave us his guarantee.

"If you don't see at least a dozen caribou a day—and I mean close, not miles away—I won't charge you for the trip."

We flew for thirty minutes before caribou appeared, scattered among the muskegs below, first in groups of a dozen or so, then in bunches of twenty, thirty, and more. Every group pointed east, noses in the wind. They were moving.

News in the Nelchina Basin travels in the wind, rain, and snow. That night, wolves howling nearby told me that the last of the caribou were passing through. Wolves can always be found on the heels of great caribou herds, picking off stragglers. A cold rain pattering on the tent fly faded, hissed, and then fell silent. The temperature had dropped, my nose was cold.

Larry had groaned the next morning when he saw the snow, huddled deeper into his sleeping bag as if it were all a cold, bad dream. I dressed warmly, picked up my rifle, and stepped outside; there was work to do and the sooner it was done, the sooner I could put down my rifle and pack and pick up the four-weight.

Hunting and fishing, when you think about it, are variations of the same theme. Both include similar elements of sport—a quest, a stalk, an engagement (providing you're skillful or lucky). But fishing's a lark. You can catch 'em and let them go, having fun without straining your back or getting your hands dirty. Of course, clean hands don't fill the freezer.

Lunch time has come and gone. I've grown impatient, cold (standing around in the snow on a wind-blown hillside will do that to you), so now I'm walking around the lake, hunting. A teal flushes from some frost-bitten sedges, but the lake is otherwise still, without ripple or riseform. Perhaps there are no fish, or maybe the season is too far gone, the water too cold. The very idea, that an unnamed lake in the center of the wilderness might have fish, would seem presumptuous anyplace else. But in Alaska, hope treads in every pond, every unfished stream. This is a place where dreamers dare and rarely go unrewarded.

A mile or so from camp, I'm entering thick timber. The taiga—a botanical edge formed where boreal forest peters out and Arctic tundra takes over—is tough to hunt. Forest, mostly willow and stunted black spruce (a big tree might stand twelve feet high), limits visibility. Caribou blend nicely into the black, gray, and white mosaic of trees and brush.

In the timber I cross tracks—plenty of them. Several bands apparently have passed without me seeing them. Not that caribou are what I would call sneaky creatures, but instinct serves them well. In open country they tend to follow subtle seams and shallow valleys that conceal them from distant, meat-hungry eyes. Timbered stretches work equally well.

I'm stumbling around in the brush, wondering what I should do to speed things up, when ivory tines appear bobbing through the trees: a band of heavy-antlered bulls. Finding an open shot is tough (I actually find myself *chasing* them, sort of like a two-legged wolf), but soon I find an opportunity and my hunt is swiftly over.

There's no sense describing the gore and drudgery that follows. Let's just say I'm happy to get the work out of the way. The
freezer will be packed with roasts and steaks and hamburger, a
fact that generates a sense of pride and security with winter coming on. The rest of the afternoon is spent high-stepping over
snow-covered tussocks to camp and back, top-heavy under
packs loaded with meat and bone, cursing softly.

Now it is evening and the air is growing colder; skins of ice are
forming in a cove near camp. I've put together my fly rod, and
since I've seen no surface activity (not a big surprise, there are no
bugs), I've decided to go with a weighted nymph. The landscape,
resting snowbound under a foundering sun, is at once striking
and peaceful. Winter already is settling in.

I'm standing in a patch of withered blueberries, casting my
heart out to a ledge where the shallows drop off into something
dark, unfathomable. I've been at it for a while—twenty minutes,
perhaps—and would be ready to call it a season, except that I'd
sensed a short pluck early on. Of course, it might have been
weeds or a beaver stick on the bottom, or even my imagination.
But it is enough to keep me out here, away from the campfire,
watching the water thicken.

I'm stripping in slowly, allowing that cold-blooded creatures
in near-freezing water might lack the zip of those in warmer
places. Then, something's knocking. I pause, start to strip in
some more, and in a flash the fish is on. The struggle is short, familiar—a muddled, head-shaking moment of mild hysteria, and
soon I'm lifting my rod high, leading the fish in among snow-
capped stones.

From camp, on a knoll above me, Larry has stopped packing
sleeping bags and tarps to look. Gently, I remove the fly and

watch the fish fade into deep water, then stand up and scan the sky for the plane. Everything is still, you can almost hear the ice forming.

In a moment I'm falsecasting again, pulling out more line. Akers will arrive to pick us up anytime, before winter really gets serious. But not before I stick one last grayling.

October Wind

Paul Cyr is a silhouette on a sunlit gravel bar, casting to a black, roiling pool where his leader, caught by the low-slung October sun, forms a halo of sparkles and flashes. Salt, decay, and the echo of waves pounding sand ride an upriver breeze.

Like a cat stalking, Paul crouches, his fly rod a feeling, probing antenna fixed deliberately over the pool. The air is tense. Suddenly, Paul's rod surges, wrenches in his hands like a writhing Dolly Varden. Green fly line snaps taut, and something downstream splashes violently. For an instant, the world spins like a top, racing ever faster, and then, in a snap of light leader, everything stops, as if someone flipped a switch.

The static is fleeting. Brief as a spark. Soon the river shuffles on, distant surf roars as before. Only Paul remains still, on the gravel bar, staring at the pool, his line limp as silk.

When we arrived early this morning, wading through predawn murk, knuckles and noses stinging, the delineation between autumn and winter was unclear. Puddles near the river shattered with every step, like crystal on concrete, yet the river, muttering darkly under a white crescent moon, jogged steadily seaward, as fluid and unencumbered as it had been when salmon arrived in June.

We'd driven half the night to get here: from my home in Wasilla, through the big city of Anchorage fifty miles south, on to Paul's place in Indian, then another 200 miles south. There had been coffee in the truck's cab, by the light of the dash, and a bladder break in Turnagain Pass. At Cooper Landing, we'd stopped at an outfitter's shack on a bank overlooking the Kenai River.

The place was closed for the season. Drift boats waited in a chain-link bullpen out back, mothballed in blue tarps, suspended from action until next summer, which, in the cold darkness, seemed a long way off.

A yellow light glowed in a window, and Paul had stepped up on the porch and rapped on the door.

"Fishin'! Open up."

Mr. Fishin', mid-fifties, patch over one eye, built like a bear, is known among Kenai River regulars as a great angler. He also is a tireless talker, who, in his lisping drawl, enjoys bragging up a good day on the river—a trait that has undoubtedly contributed to his legend.

The camp belonged to a guide named Trout (same Trout who owns a certain Wasilla cafe), but Fishin' had the run of the place, having endeared himself over the summer to one of Trout's frustrated assistants: "I was fishin' Quartz Creek an' catchin' plenty of Dollys whens I notice a couple guys fishin' 'bove me. I didn't knows then it was a guide an' a client. Well, they wasn't catchin' no fish an', after watchin' me, the guide comes down an' asks what I'm usin'. I shows him an' then I calls his client over. I gives him one of my flies an' have him cast right over there. Caught a big Dolly right off."

Fishin' invited Paul and me to stay on, fish the Kenai with him for rainbow trout and Dolly Varden. That's how he closes his season each year—casting over the pea-green glacial flow of that fish-rich river until winter shuts him down. But Paul and I declined. Time seemed to be accelerating; we had to hurry.

So now we're on our own river, a stream much smaller and darker than Fishin's Kenai, searching for fish as ephemeral and elusive as the thin slice of time that separates fall from winter. Paul, still standing on the gravel bar upstream, has collected himself and is tying on a new fly. I'm drifting an Egg-sucking Leech through a deep-bottomed run, pausing on every fourth or fifth cast to chip ice from my guides.

Already, the land—ashen, dusty, brittle—is sleeping. A meadow above the river is white, a composition of frosted grass, each blade rigid, edgy. I'm nearing the end of a drift, contemplating a sense of desperation as familiar as the season, when I lift my rod to a faint tug. Something in the run responds with a sluggish heaviness, and for an instant, I think I've found what I've come for. But soon I recognize the twisting throes of a post-spawn Dolly. Even so, I play the fish with uncommon reverence. There is every possibility that this will be my last fish of the year, and in that light, snaky char aren't so bad.

Within a week, snow will fall and darkness will gather. Paul and I, like so many Alaskans, will be reduced to bitching about the monotony of winter. (Paul, the biologist, in January: "I've been sitting on my ass for three weeks counting rockfish otoliths through a microscope. How good can life be?")

The Dolly is gone, released to the stream where it will winter before returning to the surf. The sun has risen above the naked forest, and now shines full upon us. It offers some warmth, enough to melt the ice from our guides. Paul, wrapped in a stifling combination of neoprene and polar fleece, is fishing the next run up.

I'm fishing a chute too swift for mere Dollys when, finally, it happens. The strike is violent, slashing, and before I can shout, the purple gill plates and olive dorsal of a large steelhead break the surface. For the next ten minutes, the two of us will be locked in a primal contest of panic and pursuit. Only, I know we're not playing for keeps.

Sometimes, it occurs to me that I don't really understand steelhead—mysterious trout that have evolved as salmon. I wonder: do I, as an angler, treat them as salmon or trout?

All I know for sure are the natural cycles that bind steelhead to this stream; they are the first fish to run in April, and by late October, with spawning at hand, the last to arrive. Such is the mystery and the promise that brought me here. The idea of closing the season the way it began, with the same powerful fish, is somehow irresistible, fitting.

In quiet water near the foot of the pool, the steelhead surrenders. In its eye, I can see winter's iron reflection staring back at me. For a moment, the river, the fish, and my own brooding nature seem to merge into a living painting, cold and fresh, gray and blue. Time now to let the day ferment in the mind, as the best days always do, to meld with the soul.

Winter's coming, gently as it can. You can feel it in the chill October wind.

Winter

Fishing the
Black Hole

I felt winter coming for a long, long time. Since August. No, June. Hell, May. That's a little neurotic, I know, but when you've weathered more than thirty dark seasons in southcentral Alaska, summers seem little more than fleeting reflections. Winters hang on forever, heavy and cold as frozen stone, and it gets easier to see the inevitability of the next winter from the wake of the last.

Still, even with winter constantly on the horizon, no amount of anticipation can dull the shock of that first snowfall or the first sub-zero day. Whimpering in a closet or working late at the office are pathetic forms of denial. The best way to deal with an Alaskan winter is to meet it head-on, on its own terms. And that's what I'm doing today.

Mark Kufel, six-foot, four-inches tall, face nearly covered in a frosted beaver-fur hat, is preparing our first fishing hole. There is something visceral in the action of an auger biting into a frozen lake. It's like grinding glass, with ice popping and shattering in tinkling shards. The sound is coarse, you can feel it beneath your ribs, tearing at something warm and tender.

The crystalline lake is snow-covered, surrounded by black spruce trees flocked in thick, hairy hoarfrost coats. Far below zero, the air packs a bite that is hard and metallic. Ice fog mutes the afternoon sun, lending the atmosphere a pallid, silver tone.

Mark's almost there, leaning on the auger, twisting, turning the bit ... break-through! The sound of water splashing is a contradiction to the frozen cosmos. Through the hole, a black portal to a liquid world, wafts the unmistakable fragrance of lake water. It is a summer smell, rich, sweet, suggestive of pond lilies, Labrador Tea, and trout; it carries the essence of a time, however brief, when the sun rides high and warm over a world of float tubes, craneflies dancing, and water rippling.

I suspect all ice fishermen encounter moments of truth when they ask, as I am now, *Why?* Alaska presently would not seem a hospitable place. But some creatures are born to fish, and the acts and emotions surrounding our sport define us. We are, Hemingway told us, born lucky.

I was born lucky, an angler confirmed and seasoned by age three. By age five, I knew more about the color dynamics of tannic water (like the eye of a caribou bull, it has a distinct translucent amber quality) than most men ever do and I knew about the way a grayling's purple and turquoise iridescence is lost the moment the fish dies. These things are delicate and elusive, like a scent in the summer breeze that is at once familiar, mysterious, warm, and pleasant. Children have better ears and eyes and noses for things like these—ethereal things—perhaps because they do not presume to identify and label things they do not know.

Why shiver over a frozen lake for cold fish? Because I am a man with a child's curiosity for something that lives within but that I cannot see. We do not ask why we love, because the answers get lost in the connections between our hearts and our tongues. Maybe, for the same reason, we should not ask why we fish, along dashing streams or from thick ice pans.

The first hour is broken by an occasional foot-long rainbow. The lake is a womb and from our tiny holes fish are yanked into the cold light, gaping, wet and quivering like newborns freshly delivered. When we're gone, little evidence will remain of the killing we made; just a couple of frozen craters and blood-stained ice.

Since this is the time of year when seasoned Alaskans bug out for a few weeks to Belize, Christmas Island, Maui, I'm thinking aloud of palm trees, warm surf lapping gently, geckos plastered on sun-warmed walls. Yeah, says Mark, we could be deep-sea fishing, sipping umbrella drinks, and catching wahoo or some damned thing. Why, I wonder, are they called wahoo? Maybe, Mark says, it has something to do with the heat and the drinks and the tug of huge fish in blue saltwater—add it all together and it's probably hard to keep from hollering "*Wahoo!*"

But this ain't the tropics and it's too cold to be shouting *Wahoo!* or anything else over fat little trout yanked from holes in the ice. Mark's got another bite. His red-and-white bobber breaks a skin of fresh ice, wobbles, then disappears suddenly, sloshing into the black hole. He sweeps up his rod, the short, spaghetti-thin outfit of ice-fishing for trout, and the struggle is on. Now this is a *fish*. Line peels off the reel and again I am reminded of those warmer, brighter times, of dragonflies hovering and wood frogs burping.

The fish, when it appears finally, is obese, spotted, amber-sided, nearly two feet long. It is the kind of trout I love to catch in June from my float tube. I'm standing over my own hole, watching furtively, hoping silently that he will return the trout so that the fish and I might meet again in June over a four-weight rod and light tippet. But soon the fish is flopping on the ice, body freezing instantly, death throes stiff, slowing, mechanical. Ice-fishing seems an intrinsically mercenary activity.

A coyote pack yips at precisely the place where the sun will go down minutes from now. The air seems too thin to breathe, too cold, dry and brittle to sustain life. Makes me wonder yet again what the hell I'm doing out here. Winters here can seem oppressive if you let them; so dark, cold, the snow to your thighs.

When I next look up, the trees on the far side of the lake have devoured the sun and night is sliding in like a shadow, purple and inky. This is when the final bite occurs, landlocked salmon mostly, quarter-pound slivers of chrome and flesh. By now our bones ache, the heatless ether creeping through seams and zippers; our fingers sting and I'd really rather not take off my gloves to deal with cold-blooded creatures writhing in freezing slime. But something makes me do it.

Fishing with bait through holes in the ice may not sound like a sane thing to do. But then, I've about decided that there's little sanity in an Alaskan winter. The only way to beat it is to enjoy it, and that means getting out and facing the demon.

Soon, in full darkness, we'll pack up and cross the frozen lake. Mark will go ahead, into the murky forest, out of sight. The temperature will drop and my mustache, glaciated over the day with every breath, will ride my face, a solid bar of ice. Somewhere in the stillness ahead, I'll hear Mark shuffling through the snow. And then the peace will be broken by a ragged, eerie howl: *Wahooooo!*

A Perfect World

M id-December. Alaska, the flyfisher's paradise from May
through October, seems more an angler's hell. Lakes and
streams are frozen solid, glazed hard as quartz. Have been for
nearly eight weeks and will remain so for ... well, I'd rather not
think about it. We've something around five hours of sunlight
this time of year, low, dim light at best, seeping over a frozen
horizon on bright days, little more than a vague glow.

The winter blues start here, in the wallowing darkness of the
solstice, and the only real cure is to pack up and head south.
Break time.

John Woods and I are driving in darkness, headed north of his
home in Victoria, B.C. on TransCanada 1, what locals call the
"Up-island Highway." I have cracked the passenger window to
savor December air that is fresh and mild in a pleasantly spring-
like way. Yesterday, on the flight from Alaska to Vancouver Island, I'd looked down through breaks in the clouds upon snow-
covered mountains. When we landed in Victoria, the sight of
green grass and the touch of a gentle breeze on my cheek had left
me giddy.

A definite seasonal wrinkle exists between temperate Vancouver Island and just about any other latitude north or longitude
east. Early in November, I'd phoned John from my Wasilla home
as a snowstorm, compliments of a Siberian front, added fresh
depth to the powdery foot already covering my home ground.
Only the day before, he had for fished chum salmon south of

Victoria in the Sooke River, "just for practice." He and his son
had worn out their arms battling the powerful, tiger-striped fish.
How, he'd asked, were things in Alaska?

As we drive, the air rushing through his station wagon window grows suddenly heavy, tainted with decay; it is an odor that
is both repulsive and familiar. John speaks.

"Goldstream Creek. Smell the salmon?"

I haven't smelled a salmon stream in nearly three months. He
tells me that late chum and coho entered Goldstream weeks ago.
Most have completed their life's quest and now line the stony
banks like scattered cordwood, food for scavenging eagles and
black bears. A few, he says, still whirl in the shallows, perform-
ing the final dance of the Pacific salmon, a tribute to the circle of
life and death.

Less than an hour out of Victoria, the sky turns silver and I can
see, as we race by, the hulking silhouettes of tall coastal evergreens. We are approaching the outskirts of Duncan—home of
the world's largest hockey stick, a sixty-two-meter replica poised
for a slapshot over the municipal ice arena—when Woods points
to a bridge ahead.

"There," he says, "that's the river." A band of water perhaps
four lanes wide flows by swiftly, yet smoothly, punctuated by
swirling dimples that amplify the dawn light.

Yes, that is the river—or, more accurately, one version of it. I
know, because this isn't my first glimpse of the Cowichan. In
fact, winter visits have become an annual tradition, and I've
crossed this bridge often enough to know that the Cowichan we
will fish today is a different river, narrower, wilder, dashing
around boulders.

Vancouver Island is nearly 300 miles long and spans roughly
eighty miles at its widest point, making it seem less an island than
its own small continent. There are remote reaches that require of

visiting anglers long hikes, bush plane flights, or travel by boat. Yet in its heart it is an accessible place, where highways, gravel lanes, and logging roads are carved among coastal mountains and along galloping rivers.

This time of year, as I've said, Alaskans who live to fish and who have the financial means to escape, traditionally fly south to places like Christmas Island, Belize, New Zealand, or South America; places where the sun is warm, even hot and where fish can be caught on flies. Vancouver Island is closer and home to my wife's family.

Besides, it's Christmas. The kids must visit their grandparents. And I must fish.

The island promises escape in varying degrees: wander Victoria's outskirts on spring-like December afternoons, casting off the beaches to sea-run cutthroat trout; fish for steelhead up-island in the rocky gorges of the Gold River in February; float-tube area lakes in March for fat rainbow trout.

You can return at the end of a day to a tidy bed-and-breakfast outside Port Alberni, enjoy a stout Canadian beer at a Campbell River lodge, or pamper yourself with an evening of wine and seafood at a waterfront restaurant in Victoria. Over the years, as winter snows have piled deep and life's rhythms have slowed, even threatened to stop completely, Vancouver Island has provided an escape that I've come to depend upon.

We're twenty minutes west of the giant hockey stick when John pulls his old station wagon off a logging road and into a stand of six-story-high hemlock and fir. John is retelling a tale I first heard over the phone a month earlier. It happened at "the trestle," a stretch of river below Lake Cowichan where we will fish this morning:

Warm weather had made for slow fishing and as John crossed the abandoned logging trestle to call it a day, he saw a large fish holding torpedo-like in a tailout below. The sight turned him around. He drifted several fly patterns past the indifferent fish before tying on a Doc Spratley (a move of desperation, since the Doc Spratley, imitating a dragonfly nymph or a small minnow, is probably better known as a lake pattern).

John cast far above the shadow in the current, and as his fly began to drift, he felt a light tug and realized he'd hooked a tiny fish. Suddenly, the big fish, still as a log until now, came alive. In a savage boil, it grabbed the fly and the hapless minnow impaled on it and ran in a splashing wake straight upstream. At the end of the run, the fish leaped once and John saw the ruby stripe on its side, the hawkish glare in its eye; then his line fell slack and the steelhead was gone.

"Sounds like there's a lesson in there somewhere," I reply.

"Yeah," says John. "Fish with live bait."

An opening in the trees beyond the station wagon reveals the trestle, a weathered span of rough-cut timbers that stretches to the far side of a gentle gorge seventy feet above the river. The river rushes below, dark, impatient, reflecting in dancing fractions pale gray alder trunks backed by dark conifers. The air is damp and smells of cedar, woody and slightly sour.

December on the Cowichan is not always without snow. Sometimes a dusting will come in the night, transient, flocking the evergreens, leaving the river, in contrast, steaming and sullen. Crossing the trestle at such times becomes treacherous, since felt-soled wading boots are designed to grip wet rocks, not ice- and snow-covered wood. So you focus on each step, pausing midway to peer down between the ties at the river, tiny and roaring far below, before carefully completing the journey.

I fished here once with throbbing temples on New Year's Day in four inches of snow. The river was low, many of the smaller tributaries frozen, and late cohos, purple and black, rolled in the eddies. I spent part of the day playing cat-and-mouse with a steelhead that hid in a hole beneath a washed-out root mass. Out of curiosity, I'd drifted a white Bunny Fly into the hole. When nothing happened, I began stripping in the fly and, just as the streamer cleared the edge of the roots, the head and shoulders of a heavy fish appeared. In anticipation, I tried too soon to set the hook and missed the strike. I let the water rest for a while, but the fish was spooked and never struck again.

The trestle crossing today isn't bad, since this December there is no snow, and soon I'm standing on a mat of green sphagnum overlooking a pool. A great blue heron lands heavily on a fir branch—an unlikely perch for a spear-headed, stick-legged wading bird—and settles in to watch. John is fishing downriver when I begin casting at the tail of the pool. It feels nice to have escaped winter, and there is a certain catharsis in the rhythmic spring of a six-weight rod and the slickness of fresh water beaded on floating line. At the end of my third drift, I sense a sharp pluck, then nothing. I retrieve the fly and cast again, crouching slightly, focused this time, like the heron, on every inch of my drift.

I can see my streamer, a purple shadow in the off-green current, as it swings to the drift's end. The fly hangs there briefly, and then a silhouette darts into view and tackles it. For a moment there is nothing else in the world but a thrashing fish, a river, and a taut line connecting me to it all. Then the part of me that yearns desperately to hold and study wet, quivering fish—to count coup like a plains warrior of the Old West—urges me to horse the fish, to cut the battle short. But I choose instead to savor the moment, leading the fish, as its strength dissipates, eventually to calm water at the river's edge.

When, as a prisoner of an Alaskan winter, you haven't held a fish for a quarter of a year, it is difficult not to shamelessly share your reprieve with all who will listen. I whoop like a kid, or a warrior counting coup, but John has fished his way out of sight. Even the heron has gone, and, in a way, it pleases me to know that I might as well be the last man on earth.

The trout—a cutthroat seventeen inches long—gasps and the gill plates flare, displaying broad orange stripes under each side of the jaw. I hold the trout in the current, then let go and watch it vanish into the pool.

For many, flyfishing's appeal seems linked directly to the energy and variances of current, and that's fine. Yet the world sets no better stage for reflection, and often fantastic action, than a windless lake. Vancouver Island's scores of lakes range from more than twenty miles long to tranquil potholes surrounded by moss-bearded old growth. One of my most pleasant moments was a misty morning spent in a canoe on Durrance Lake outside Victoria, casting among rising cutthroat and rainbow trout. Many Victoria-area lakes also have smallmouth bass, introduced early in the century. Up-island, the lakes become too cool for bass, hosting instead Dolly Varden, along with cutts and rainbow trout.

For different sport and scenery, rich saltwater fisheries surrounding the island also are worth exploring. Gary Bruce, a Victoria mechanic addicted to the kick of fast cars and bucking seas, once invited me deep sea fishing off the coast west of Nitinat Lake. We launched Gary's seventeen-foot Bayliner into the head of the lake and cruised more than ten miles to the outlet, a short, violent neck of tidally influenced river that plunges into the open Pacific Ocean.

Gary prefers saltwater fishing and avidly trolls for feeder

springs—immature king salmon—and cohos. But that day our quest was halibut. We jigged large, heavy spoons over deep water, and often before our hooks touched bottom, fish would be on our lines. We caught black sea bass, yellow-eyed red rockfish (locally called red snapper), ling cod, and just about every other type of bottom fish except halibut. Gary has since done well on halibut in the area, but we hauled anchor a little early that day—tall Pacific swells sometimes have an unspeakable effect on the equilibrium of landlubbing flyfishers and ... let's just say that I've never been seasick riding the film of placid lakes or wading feral rivers.

John Woods, a self-described "old hippie"—complete with ponytail, mustache, and granny glasses—finds poetry in good wine, unique pottery glazes, and the gonzo rantings of Hunter S. Thompson. Too, he covets the places where trout are found, whether those places be rivers, lakes, or Vancouver Island estuaries where sea-run cutthroat trout feed. Two years ago, John led me to an estuary minutes from downtown Victoria where a brook less than three feet wide fed into a lapping barnacle- and mussel-encrusted bay.

Days earlier, John had fished the estuary with my father-in-law for silver-bright, sea-run cutts. Each man employed his preferred equipment: John casting streamers with a light fly rod, Walt a flashy spinner on a short rod and open-face reel. In the end, the spinning outfit's far-reaching casting advantage paid off in the form of a couple of fat, fourteen- and sixteen-inch cutts. John couldn't quite reach the fish.

Hemlock- and cedar-lined, underscored by a rocky beach reminiscent of the classic seaside escapes of Carmel or Big Sur, the estuary was a quiet, scenic place. But John and I, stubborn flyfishers to the end, caught no fish that day. Instead we spent a pleasant afternoon casting flies to cutthroats that leapt out of reach and watching flocks of buffleheads and goldeneyes sweep across the bay like feathered bullets.

Today, on the Cowichan, I am catching fish. It is a lovely river, with lovely fish and a bucolic serenity that I've enjoyed since the first time I visited it. The late Roderick Haig-Brown, Vancouver Island angler and author, wrote in his classic, *A River Never Sleeps*: "One may love a river as soon as one sets eyes upon it; it may have certain features that fit instantly with one's conception of beauty, or it may recall the qualities of some other river, well known and deeply loved."

The Cowichan, however, is only one of many gorgeous Vancouver Island streams. Others include Haig-Brown's own Campbell, the Gold, Big and Little Qualicum, and the Salmon. This promise of bright, new water led me one year ago to the Stamp River near Port Alberni.

Haig-Brown had written of fishing for steelhead on the Stamp with his good friend General Money. John and I, without a map, but with Haig-Brown's offhand directions in mind, spent a day exploring the Stamp by driving logging roads that parallel the river's course. It was a damp, sulky day, and we did not fish as hard as we would have liked, but we did, along with several locals, find "Money's Pool."

The pool is incredibly deep, abysmal, resting nervously at the foot of a rocky cascade. Steelhead fresh from the sea stack up along the bottom of the pool, waiting until nightfall to continue upstream to spawning grounds. By the time John and I found the place, the hour was late and we were forced to leave, skunked, after a short time. Back at the car, a gray-haired Asian man who said he was from the city of Vancouver stopped by.

"S'cuse me," he said politely. I turned from slipping my rod into its case and saw the man, slightly hunched, gripping by the gills an eight-pound steelhead buck. "S'cuse me. Can you tell me what kind of fish is this?"

I glanced at John, who stood slack-jawed on the far side of the station wagon.

"Yes," I said, "that's a steelhead."

The man's face brightened. "Good! This is what I want. Thank you."

Before he left, he told me he had caught the fish on a fresh prawn in Money's Pool.

Back on the Cowichan, a fish as long as my arm swirls near the surface at the end of my drift. My heart pounds. It may have been an old coho in dark spawning colors—I caught one soon after that first cutthroat. Or it may have been a steelhead. Surrounded by current, green trees, and gentle air, I cast again, focused on the moment, ready for a strike and that electric surge that keeps me fishing. For now, I've found a pleasing balance, between my frozen home and my need to fish twelve months a year. It is, if only for an instant, a perfect world.